Today's Top SURFBOARDS

ROD SUMPTER

Schiffer Publishing Ltd
4880 Lower Valley Road Atglen, Pennsylvania 19310

All valuations are by the author and are based on what a surfboard might procure at auction in 2007. However, please note that the bidding process can produce huge variations with regard to final price. If details of images were not supplied by the manufacturer, the accompanying dimensions, dates, and values have been prepared by the author as a guide. Text for Chuck Bassett Surfboards written by the author from Chuck Bassett's extensive notes. Values in this book do not represent the current cost of replacement or manufacture.

The author assumes no liability for valuations, accidents to, or injuries sustained by readers participating in activities described in this book.

Other Schiffer Books by Rod Sumpter
Surf Art! Graphics and Memorabilia

Other Schiffer Books on Related Subjects
Surf's Up: Collecting the Longboard Era, by Mark Blackburn
Surfing, by Nancy N. Schiffer in cooperation with San Francisco Airport Museums
Hula Girls and Surfer Boys, by Mark Blackburn
Hawaiiana: The Best of Hawaiian Design, by Mark Blackburn

Library of Congress Control Number: 2007925675

Designed by John P. Cheek
Cover design by Bruce Waters
Type set in Zurich Blk BT/News Gothic BT

ISBN: 978-0-7643-2764-3
Printed in China

Published by Schiffer Publishing Ltd.
4880 Lower Valley Road
Atglen, PA 19310
Phone: (610) 593-1777; Fax: (610) 593-2002
E-mail: Info@schifferbooks.com

For the largest selection of fine reference books on this and related subjects, please visit our web site at **www.schifferbooks.com**
We are always looking for people to write books on new and related subjects. If you have an idea for a book please contact us at the above address.

This book may be purchased from the publisher.
Include $3.95 for shipping.
Please try your bookstore first.
You may write for a free catalog.

In Europe, Schiffer books are distributed by
Bushwood Books
6 Marksbury Ave.
Kew Gardens
Surrey TW9 4JF England
Phone: 44 (0) 20 8392-8585; Fax: 44 (0) 20 8392-9876
E-mail: info@bushwoodbooks.co.uk
Website: www.bushwoodbooks.co.uk
Free postage in the U.K., Europe; air mail at cost.

Contents

Acknowledgments

This book would not have been possible without the support, help, and enthusiasm of my wife Valerie, who checked the manuscript and looked over me while I was surfing. Thanks to my son John and his wife Sarah, and to baby Ben and Lucy who light up our lives. To John, a triple thanks for his fantastic deep barrel surfing and advice throughout this book and for keeping watch over me on many a dangerous photo shoot. His surfing is my inspiration.

Thanks to Chris and Liz for travel information and to Mum who was always there. And to Chuck Bassett, Drew Brophy, Darren Handley, Len Dibben, G. MacDuff, Gul International Ltd., Kimo Greene, Robb Havassy, Todd Proctor, Josh Dowling, Gil Talamantes, Charlie Bunger, Mark and Renae Lani Anderson, John E. Baxendale, Seabase Ltd., Bill Yates, Tim Bessell, and Graham Looker. And for inspiration, Mick Mabbott, Davey Jones, Dennis White, Bob Head, Tigger Newling, Kevin Cavey, Julian Charlton, and Ray Morton.

And a warm thanks to all those who deserve to be in the book that I have forgotten.

Introduction

I started shaping as a kid, beginning with aeroplanes made of balsa wood, moving on to a slingshot crafted from the fork of a tree, then to a bow and arrow, and finally—when the great Hawaiian surfing team led by Duke Kahanmoku gave an epic exhibition at Avalon, Sydney in 1957, the crowd going wild with excitement—I progressed to shaping my first surfboard.

Achieving the optimum shape in all these things was a challenge, and the use of light and shadows became the whittler's best friend. By arranging lighting to cast a shadow across a piece of wood, I found the tool that is the truest means of sculpturing perfection. There, in the dim light of dawn and dusk, long shadows in the shed my father had built for repairing boards helped me create a true, clean 10' board.

Today's modern shaping room benefits from the same use of lights and shadows—it's a lot like whittling in sunset lighting. Light causes a deepening shadow to appear along a curve, which shows a straight line better than any other measuring method. In a shaper's tool box are templates, electric planers, wire mesh, fine grit sandpaper, small hand planers the size of a finger, and, of course, artificial lighting set-ups with florescent tubes.

I build surfboards today and have worked in surfboard factories for years, and I love the lifestyle, the dedication, the endless evolution of creating. When I'm in the glossing room masking up a full board union jack flag in red, white, and blue, I feel inspired. The first union jack flagged board I took to the 1966 World Surfing Championships was wrapped around top and bottom and it got me 5th place in San Diego over all in the entire world! Yes, I did surf well, but I had created the first design to woo judges—and none of them missed a single wave I caught because of the board's colour and style.

To me, a surfboard is a surfer's best friend; it's the apple of one's eye and a window to the surfer's future skill and achievements a ticket to the best show on earth! As a piece of equipment, the surfboard is as precise as a Swiss watch made to the spec of a dolphin's shape speeding in the ocean—every tiny cell and curve has a function. The board's performance is analogous to that of a favourite cue, dart, arrow, javelin or spear, but my favourite image—one I visualize every time I'm ready to tackle and carve the smallest and biggest waves the ocean can muster—is of a sword or blade.

All of the surfboards shown in this book are hand crafted custom boards and some have become moulded for high volume production. The artwork on custom built boards can be truly amazing, and the fantastic painting and spraying adds meaning and enjoyment to one's best friend.

Ordering a custom board is about speaking to a shaper, telling him or her about your current board, and discussing your surfing. It's a fine-tuned process. This book shows the scope of custom surfboards and the beauty that shapers and artists achieve in making them. Many board-building friends from around the world have contributed wonderful surfboard images showing their talent and love of building surfboards.

Truly good surfing is a creative thing…it's a gift. On a really good day, when you're surfing to the limits on the best waves in the world, riding on the edge of pure performance, and experiencing the ultimate harmony, you have to thank your surfboard—it shares the wave with you, and that gift you've found is priceless.

—Rod Sumpter

USA

Balsa Bill Surfboards

Photo courtesy of Balsa Bill Yerkes.

9'8", balsa pintail, 2005. $2500.

Photo courtesy of Balsa Bill Yerkes.

9'11", balsa square tail, 2005. $2500.

Photo courtesy of Balsa Bill Yerkes.

10' Mal, 2004. $2600.

Photo courtesy of Balsa Bill Yerkes.

Balsa Bill and Nola, Waikiki. Only the best balsa wood is used in the traditional hot dog style board made famous by Waikiki beach boys at Diamond Head. 2005. $3900.

Photo courtesy of Balsa Bill Yerkes.

A balsa board in progress, 2005.

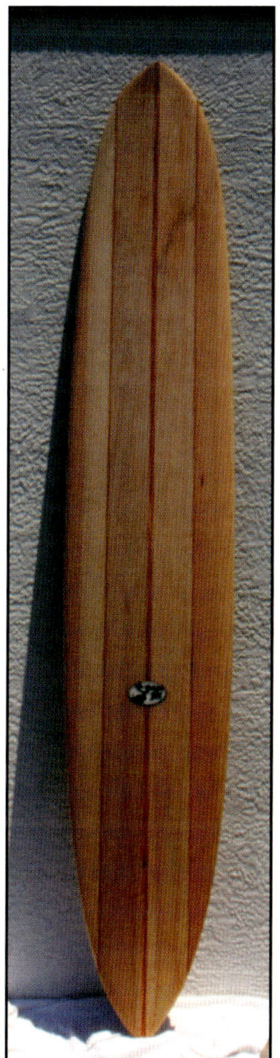

Photo courtesy of Balsa Bill Yerkes.

9’10”, triple stringer, 2006. $3000.

Photo courtesy of Balsa Bill Yerkes.

Balsa laminated fin, 2005. $125.

Robb Havassy Surfboards

Photo courtesy of Robb Havassy, www.havassyart.com

6'4", 2005. $1000.

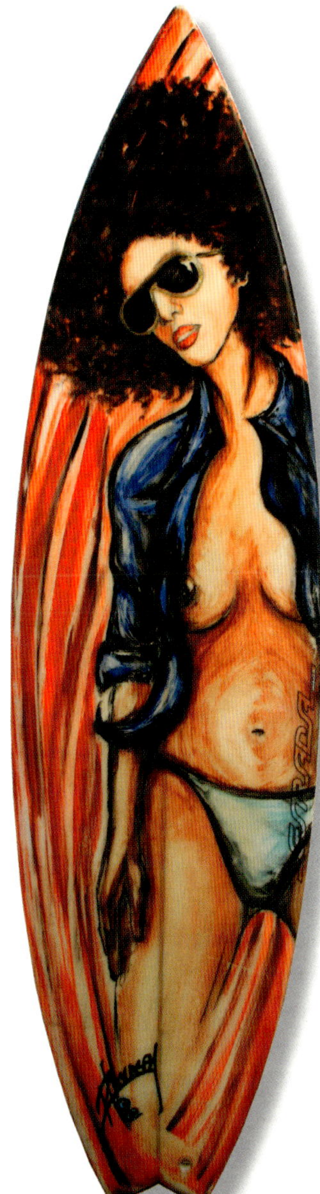

Photo courtesy of Robb Havassy, www.havassyart.com

6', Vanessa, 2004. $1200.

Photo courtesy of Robb Havassy, www.havassyart.com

6'3", 2004. $1100.

Photo courtesy of Robb Havassy. www.havassyart.com

6'2", Daisy board, 2005. $1400.

6'4", NY Kiss, 2005. $3500.

Photo courtesy of Robb Havassy, www.havassyart.com

6'4", Kiss board, 2005. $2200.

Photo courtesy of Robb Havassy, www.havassyart.com

6'6", Lotus, 2005. $1600.

Photo courtesy of Robb Havassy, www.havassyart.com

6', 2004. $2500.

Photo courtesy of Robb Havassy, www.havassyart.com

6'6", 2004. $1500.

Photo courtesy of Robb Havassy, www.havassyart.com

Photo courtesy of Robb Havassy, www.havassyart.com

Three boards, 2005. $2000-$3000.

Photo courtesy of Robb Havassy, www.havassyart.com

Robb Havassy at work.

John Sumpter at Pinballs.

Proctor Surfboards

Photo courtesy of Todd Proctor, Proctor Surfboards.

6'4", 2003. $400.

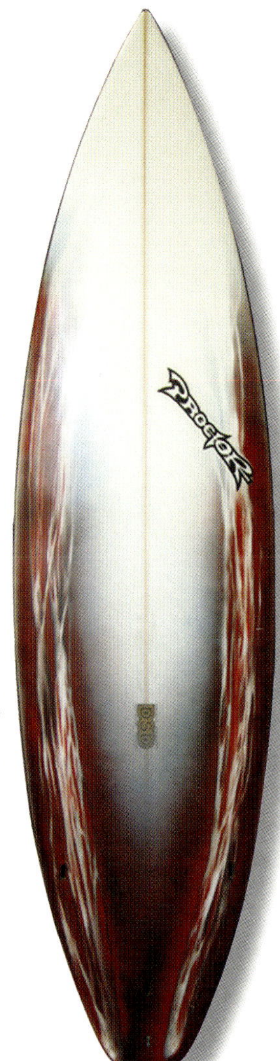

Photo courtesy of Todd Proctor, Proctor Surfboards.

6'5", 2004. $600.

Photo courtesy of Todd Proctor, Proctor Surfboards.

6'6", 2005. $600.

Photo courtesy of Todd Proctor, Proctor Surfboards.

6'3", 2004. $900.

Photo courtesy of Todd Proctor, Proctor Surfboards.

6'5", 2005. $900.

Photo courtesy of Todd Proctor, Proctor Surfboards.

9', 2005. $900.

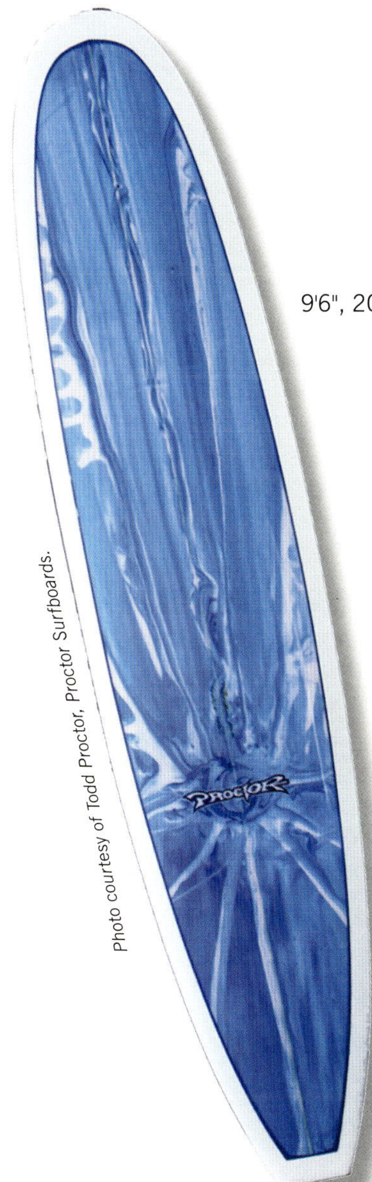

Photo courtesy of Todd Proctor, Proctor Surfboards.

9'6", 2004. $900.

Photo courtesy of Todd Proctor, Proctor Surfboards.

6', 2004. $400.

Proctor Surfboards catalogue.

*FIN OPTIONS:
All major fin systems & glass-ons available
*COLOR OPTIONS:
Custom artwork available on all boards

Twinny Fish

They're back 'cause they're fast. This is a tribute of sorts to a very innovative design for its day; the original "Fish". A 70's style retro design, it features a rolled, almost panel vee in the nose to a slight double concave through the belly with soft chimes along the rail line. Spiral vee accelerates through the fins and out the back. Deep, wide swallowtail. Why?...For the enjoyment of hair raising lateral speed runs.

EXPERIENCE: INTERMEDIATE TO ADVANCED

The "Ridiculous" Small Wave Wonder

I almost named this board "the screamer" 'cause it speeds so fast you gotta' scream; however, I decided on "The Ridiculous" because it looks ridiculous. This is a retro-style shape with supa-fat jumbo-angled rails, a flat deck, spiral vee bottom, twin fin set-up, and a little butt tail to top it off. If you want to go retro-speeding in gutless mush, then tap into "The Ridiculous" Small Wave Wonder! Also can be set up as a single fin with removable side fins.

EXPERIENCE: INTERMEDIATE TO ADVANCED

The Module

Idea taken from the escape pod used by the droids at the beginning of Star Wars. A small wave "cheeter" board with all the trim speed and carry through the flats necessary to blow up crumblers. Utilizes single-to-double concaves to pronounced concave vee through the tail. Ridden 3-5 inches shorter, 3/4" to one inch wider, and 1/8" – 1/4" thicker than your normal board.

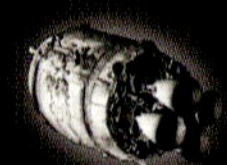

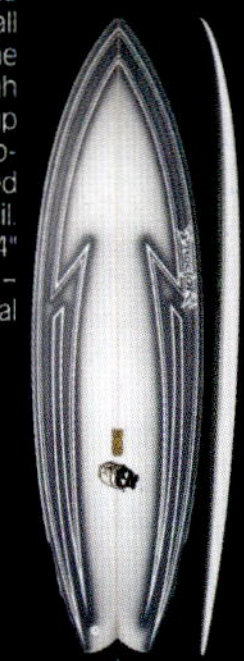

EXPERIENCE: INTERMEDIATE TO ADVANCED

Greased Pig

...So slippery, can't catch it... Designed for performance surfing in between swells. Concaves all the way through...deepest at the fins... keeps it running fast in the small stuff. Stinger swallowtail makes for more pronounced hip and pivot point to release water and increase looseness. Uses boxy rails to push back in turns. Everything the high performance shortboards do in the good waves this board does in the crud. Ridden 3-4 inches shorter and 1/4" to 1/2" wider.

EXPERIENCE: INTERMEDIATE TO ADVANCED

LeVee (Low Entry with Vee)

A speed machine for chest high waves and smaller; This is the type of board that you drive like a race car...it's speeding so all you gotta' do is hang on and steer. It has a low entry rocker for quick paddling, ease catching waves, and increased lift in small/flatter faced waves. The bottom has a single concave that transitions into a pronounced spiral vee that carries off the tail. This hull design carries excellent trim speed and gives the tail a very free feeling in the small stuff. The rails are fuller and boxier with forgiving edges that are softly blended into the bottom. You can ride this board 2-3 inches shorter, 1/2" – 3/4" wider, and 1/8" thicker than your standard shortboard.

EXPERIENCE: INTERMEDIATE TO ADVANCED

Guided Missile (Tow-in)

A tow-in board for yanking into monsters. Made from super high-density "tow weight" foam. Glassed with three layers of 6oz. S-glass both sides, double 1/4" T-band spruce stringers, and double foiled G-10 tow-in fins, weighted down to stay in the wave face at high speeds and to slingshot like a "guided missile". Bottom features a heavy concave for maximum acceleration and hold. Sizes range from 5'8" – 7'0" with widths around 16" and thicknesses around 2". All tow-in boards customized according to locations to be surfed.

EXPERIENCE: EXPERT

Groveler IV.sw (small waves)

The Groveler IV.sw has the same rocker and bottom contours as the Groveler IV.p (performance model), but uses a fuller outline and boxier rails to push back and accelerate on the small-scale days. A wider nose and tail give the board more planing area which in turn creates more lift and speed through the flat spots. The fuller, boxy rails push back so you can drive through your turns even when the waves offer little to no push. A great summer board or if you want to rip 2 foot windswell slop. I recommend a swallowtail for a looser skatier feel, or a wide squash for a raily bucketer.

EXPERIENCE: INTERMEDIATE TO ADVANCED

Flexible Epoxy Series

Picture how a dolphin moves through the water; its body in a constant state of torque and acceleration - This same concept drives the "Flexible Epoxy" technology. The boards flex when you lay into 'em and spring-back through turns, creating a sling shot effect. In development for the last five years, this unique patent pending process yields a super light, significantly stronger board with increased buoyancy. This is not a molded board; a 100% custom designed and shaped creation made in the land of the free; built around the surfer i.e. type of waves, experience, height, weight, surfing style, etc....

*All board models available in any dimensions or design.

EXPERIENCE: INTERMEDIATE TO ADVANCED

The "Blackbird"

A spry, lively bugger of a backfoot board. Developed around San Clemente's variety of waves; goes mental in points, reefs, and beachbreaks alike. Heavy single concave through the tail makes this board really alive in the pocket. It will release out the back and re-engage for fins-free type of maneuvers, airs and reverses. Designed for the new order of surfing.

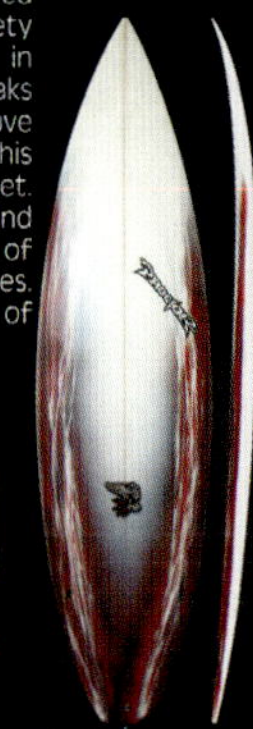

EXPERIENCE: EXPERT

Groveler IV.P (performance)

My most versatile high performance shortboard. This is a very fast design that generates it's own speed when it's small, yet holds in and rails tight arcs in the pocket when it's overhead. The rocker has a flatter area between the feet combined with an even, flowing single-to-inset double concave bottom. This creates a rail line that runs straighter from under the front foot to the lead-in fins, giving the board quick bursts of speed and incredible drive around sections. There's a fair amount of tail rocker and release coming off the back fin allowing for lightening quick, explosive turns.

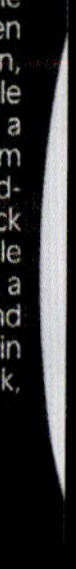

EXPERIENCE: INTERMEDIATE TO ADVANCED

Ante Up

For when the waves are getting a bit bigger and punchier than your regular shortboard can handle. The Ante Up is that little extra you need to get into bigger waves easier and maintain the balance of speed and stability necessary to rip on the overhead dream days. The rocker has an even bend from nose to tail. The bottom features a slight single-to-double concave bottom with a touch of subtle vee off the back fin for drive and a positive hold through turns. The deck is a bit more domed and foiled down to the rail. This keeps most of the volume of the board under the chest for paddling while keeping a lower volume fine-tuned rail for responsiveness. Thumbtails and rounded pins handle the power best.

All guns customized according to locations to be surfed. →

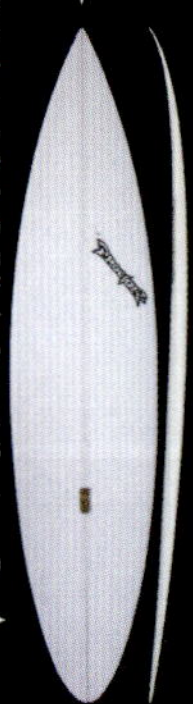

EXPERIENCE: INTERMEDIATE TO ADVANCED

Pipecleaner

This is a specialty board for thick overhead barrels. Great board for North Shore and heavy beachbreak and reefbreak travel destinations. Board features a bendy rocker to feel right at home in the pocket and deep in the pit. The deck is domed, keeping most of the volume of the board under the feet and chest with a foiled, sensitive rail. This allows for good paddling while maintaining a quick, responsive rail. I recommend a round pin or pulled-in swallowtail.

EXPERIENCE: INTERMEDIATE TO ADVANCED

West Peak

A gun for double overhead and bigger; typically a travel board unless you live in Mainland Mexico, the North Shore, or somewhere like that. Perfect for the days where the playing field is large-scale and there's a lot of water moving. The West Peak surfs top-to-bottom like a shortboard while maintaining the paddling and stability necessary to get into the waves early and drive hard turns in maxxing conditions.

Honed on the North Shore and mainland Mexico. . . this gun makes normal "survival" conditions a ripfest of larger than life proportions.

EXPERIENCE: ADVANCED

The "Howitzer" - Big Gun

For as big of waves as you dare to paddle into A Waimea, Todos Santos, Mavericks style gun . . . for deep water big wave spots.

Made with plenty of volume for paddle speed to get in early, a rocker to handle long, steep drops and a vee bottom that bolts, driving through perilous troughs.

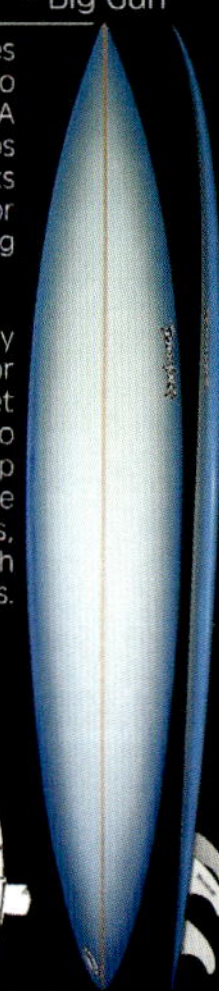

EXPERIENCE: ADVANCED TO EXPERT

Manatee

This squatty little pudge is so fun to ride!! I came up with this design one evening while I was sleeping; dreaming of surfing... a small, sectiony, mushy pointbreak....and I was having fun... and I was riding this weird looking board (which has come to be known as the manatee). In this dream I was coming off the bottom and into the lip like I was riding a shortboard, but then through the flat spots I'd walk the nose like a longboard...only it was a small board. The dream has become reality- The manatee is basically my high performance longboard with two-to-three feet of the middle cut out (average size 6'0" – 7'0"). You can ride this board off the tail like a shortboard or ride the nose like a longboard. Also sometimes referred to as the duck-billed platypus, this is a rare and odd species that enjoys itself simply because it does not take itself too seriously. Available in squashtail, swallowtail and double ender style round tail.

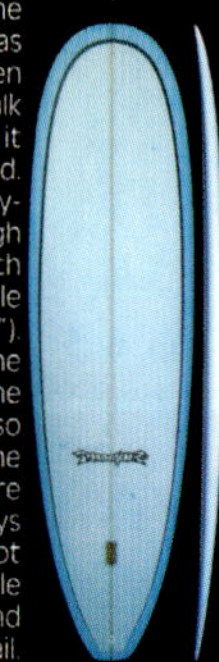

EXPERIENCE: BEGINNER TO ADVANCED

Mini Longboard

All of the longboard line is available as a scaled-down model for smaller surfers or kids. The average longboard at 9'0" x 22 1/4" x 2 7/8" is too big for a lot of kids to even get under their arm and scary to have coming back at them when they take a spill.
For petite ladies the mini-longboard is easier to manage and maneuver. The board featured here is 7'6" x 21" x 2 1/2" and perfectly suits the 75-120 lb surfer. This board rips!

EXPERIENCE: BEGINNER TO ADVANCED

rca '86 (80's Model)

you believe there is actually 80's model...I'm feeling old. tually, I was a grom in the s and what a great time it s; in part due to board sign – less work for more eed, surfing didn't have to be technical back then and it med like there were fewer e injuries... Features flat k, angled down rails, flat-to- bottom, even a beautifully eous beek nose. So here's quick, forgiving little gem t hearkens back to the days Curren and Occy duals, ng", "Rabbit", "The Saint", a ng "Butto", "The Law"... terday's heroes that aren't different from today's. mes complete with variety of style spray jobs on request.

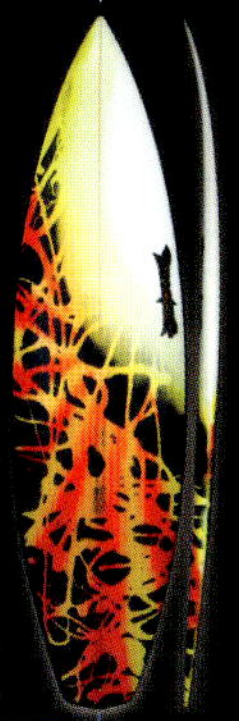

ERIENCE: INTERMEDIATE TO ADVANCED

Single Twin

A retroactive 70's style design that can be ridden as a single fin, twin fin or combination of the two i.e. single fin, single fin with small side-biters, twin fin, large twins with small center fin, etc... It is an incredibly quick and free-riding little plug. The shape is your basic 70's staple with contemporary hull contours for increased horsepower under the hood. You don't have to bear down on this board for it to push back...just ease in, sit back and enjoy freedom. Keep in mind this board is not designed for squaring off the bottom, going upside down and blowing fins out the back... The change-up is a refreshing "speed and swoop" approach. Greenough flex fin with a diamond tail rules this board.

EXPERIENCE: INTERMEDIATE TO ADVANCED

D.Y.L. (Drivey yet Loose) "Quad Fin"

What is better than a really drivey board that is still loose? – Nothing; that's the perfect combo. The board featured here with the quad fin set-up is the perfect summertime board; fuller outline to power drive you through the small-scale stuff. The quad fin set-up is available on any shape, so don't feel limited...go ahead and try it, you'll like it. The key to the whole concept is the fin placement – No back fin reduces drag while the two side fins work with the rail line and rocker to throttle you through turns. Swap out your v-6 for a v-8 under the hood with a D.Y.L. quad-fin set-up.

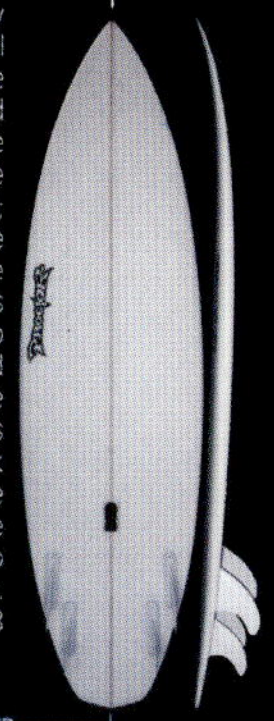

EXPERIENCE: INTERMEDIATE TO ADVANCED

6 Channel Single Fin

This board has the free riding drive of a retro single fin combined with the performance features of a modern board. It uses a flat bottom with double barrel concaves under the front foot and channels out the back for speed and drive. The progressive rocker allows for modern style top-to-bottom surfing. If you like the feel of drawing clean, long-driving bottom turns then you will love this board.

EXPERIENCE: INTERMEDIATE TO ADVANCED

Small Wave Destroyer

This is a fast running rail-to-rail board for waves ranging from knee high up to head high. It has a low entry rocker for quick paddling & early entry into waves. It has a smooth, flowing rocker bend from nose to tail; no nose or tail kick in the bottom curve. The wide point in the outline is moved forward which gives the board a fast driving, rail-to-rail, pockety feel even in the small stuff. It features a fuller nose & tail outline for increased lift & carry through flat spots.

EXPERIENCE: INTERMEDIATE TO ADVANCED

l Caves II

s shape has been refined m feedback at Australia's er Bank, Burleigh Heads and a. This board loves the rel and loves to gouge. The ker features a fair amount bend between the feet, low concaves through the and slight vee running off tail. If you want a board t throttles you maching out deep caverns, and enjoy ning a rail bucketing ough vert benders...then is the one for you.

ERIENCE: ADVANCED

Superbank

This is a specialty board designed for one type of wave – hollow, punchy grinders. It features a lot of rocker throughout and a single concave running the length of the bottom. It proves to be the fastest, most responsive board for surfing top-to-bottom and in the pocket of waves of consequence. The extreme rocker in this board bends it perfectly into tight lipped situations allowing one to play where many might otherwise stray.

EXPERIENCE: ADVANCED

SR71

Features single-to-double concave bottom for a drivey, predictable feel. Lower entry allows you to get into waves early and gain quick bursts of speed down the line. Good amount of tail rocker bending through the second half of the board makes for a tight turning, top-to-bottom board. Drives off the bottom like a dream and carries its speed through turns. An all around performance design that pushes back in waves large and small! My personal favorite.

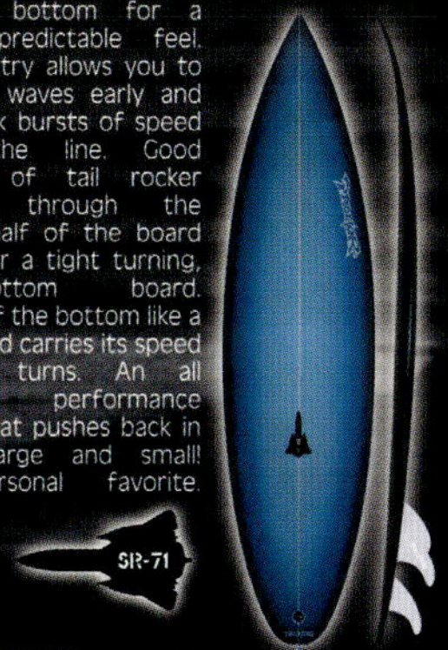

EXPERIENCE: ADVANCED

Big Chief

Developed specifically for heavier surfers and/or those that surf more off their rail; this is the shortboard you can rip on and not sink on. Heavier surfers tend to surf more with their rails then off their fins. So the fuller rails of this design are essential for a board that "pushes back" and drives through turns. Increased volume, especially under the chest, affords ease in paddling. A versatile rocker and a single-to-double concave bottom generates incredible speed in the small stuff, yet maintains the essential responsiveness for quick direction changes in the pocket. There's a slight vee off the back fin that gives the board a positive directional hold through turns.

EXPERIENCE: INTERMEDIATE TO ADVANCED

Funshape

A great board for the surfer who wants the paddling ease of a longer board with the responsiveness of a shorter board. A good beginner board; or for the surfer making the transition from longboard to shortboard; or for those who don't want to resort to a longboard, but are finding their shortboard is getting to be more work than fun. Designed to remain loose and responsive.

Also available is our High Performance Funboard. This design constitutes a sleeker outline and performance rocker to allow for quicker direction changes in and around the critical parts of the wave.

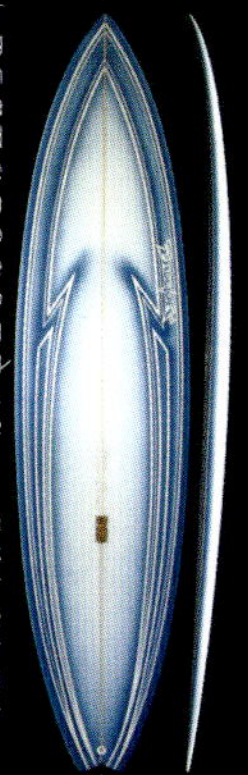

EXPERIENCE: BEGINNER TO ADVANCED

High Performance

The performance longboard features additional rocker, sleeker outline, and tapered responsive rails. The bottom utilizes a concave in the nose for increased lift in noseriding, which transitions to a double concave through the mid-section of the board, then to a concave vee or "spiral vee" through the fins and last 1/3 of the board. Everyone loves this ride!

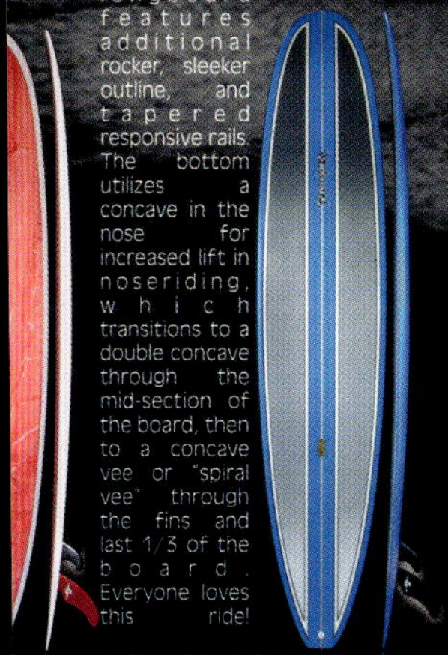

EXPERIENCE: BEGINNER TO ADVANCED

Performance Noserider

This board features a teardrop outline with a fuller nose to provide drive up front. A lower entry rocker and increased tail rocker keep it quick-trimming off the nose, yet loose off the tail. The bottom has a single concave under the nose that splits into double caves through the mid, and accelerates into a spiral vee through the last third of the board. A beveled/chimed rail releases the compressed water from underneath the board giving you a drivey, yet forgiving feel. This bottom configuration puts a V-8 under the hood when you're up on the nose, and tips the rail into throttling cutbacks. The best in the line for combining high performance responsiveness with long-time noserides. For all-around I recommend a squashtail; And for the bowlier stuff, a round pin flows.

EXPERIENCE: BEGINNER TO ADVANCED

Classic Longboard

Well . . . they're classic – 50/50 rails, rolled vee bottom, scoop in the nose; Built for trim speed, walking the nose, drop knee turns...it's a mellower era and the mood is flowin'. We do them with volan cutlaps, paddle patches, cloth inlays, acid splashes, resin swirls, tail blocks, nose blocks, pigment opques, tints, pinline art, gloss & polish... you name it we do it (even step decks...shhh – don't tell anybody).

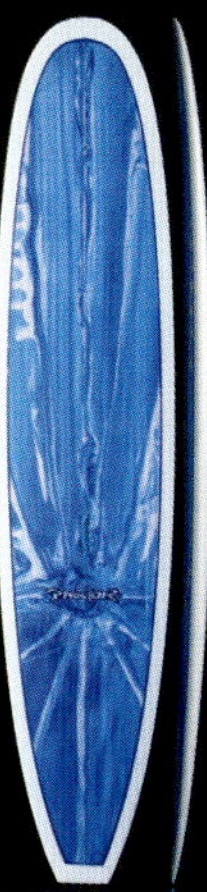

EXPERIENCE: BEGINNER TO ADVANCED

Classic Noserider

Same like wut 'da Classic Longboard..... but with a teardrop outline and a fuller nose; designed for tip time in the classic sense. Features 50/50 rails, rolled vee bottom, scoop in the nose; built for trim speed and dangling toes. Also available with volan cutlaps, knee paddle patches, cloth inlays, acid splashes, resin swirls, tail blocks, nose blocks, pigment opaques, tints, pinline art, gloss and polish.... you name it we do it. Get one...or a quiver of 'em!

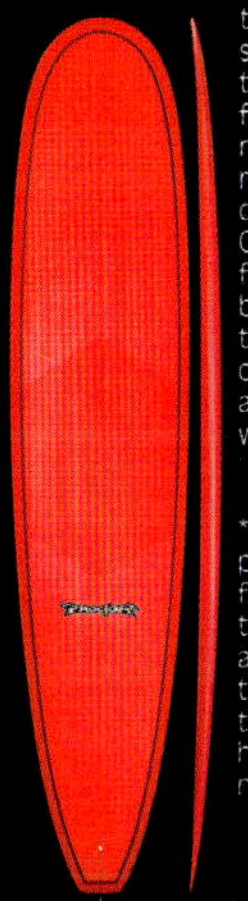

EXPERIENCE: BEGINNER TO ADVANCED

Rocket 88

A board that uses it's extra weight to drive it into sweeping bottom turns, and uses a fast rocker and no-catch 50/50 rails to bolt clean down the line. Convex over the fin transitions the board from rail-to-rail in committed speed arcs. And that's what the 'Rocket 88' is all about.

**Check out proctorsurf.com for the rest of this board's story, an interesting tale 'bout an old time ripper and his quest for a new magic stick...

EXPERIENCE: BEGINNER TO ADVANCED

The Vintage

This is a tribute to the late 50s early 60s longboards. The "Vintage" harkens back to a golden era gone by. Great for trim style surfing, smooth arcing, crop knee rail transitions, and noseriding. Also doubles as fine art and makes a beautiful wall hanger . . .for the living room, game room, or beach house.

Features 50/50 rails, rolled vee bottom, glassed on laminated wood fin, volan lay-up with cut-laps, knee paddle patch, gloss & polish. Can also be ordered with Hawaiian print floral cloth inlays, laminated wood nose/tail blocks, resin swirls, tints and opaques.

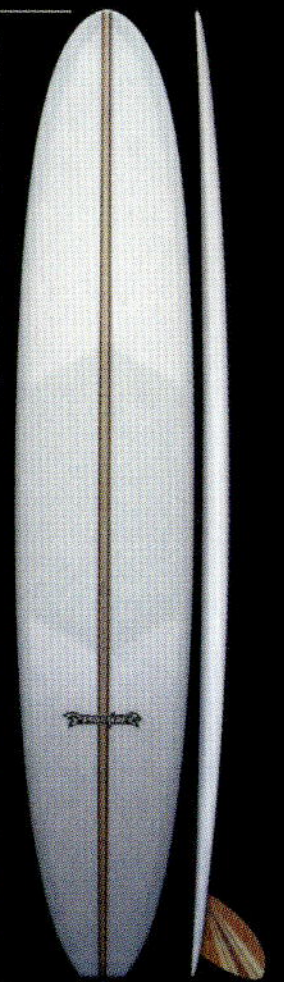

EXPERIENCE: BEGINNER TO ADVANCED

Photo courtesy of Todd Proctor, Proctor Surfboards.

Photo courtesy of Todd Proctor, Proctor Surfboards.

6'4", swallow tail, 2005. $1000.

Photo courtesy of Todd Proctor, Proctor Surfboards.

6', diamond tail, 2002. $300.

Clean close-out, John Sumpter.

Chuck Bassett Surfboards

Chuck Bassett Surfboards exemplifies the best in traditional surfboard making. Although we like to look back to the original surfing creations that our forefathers rode, the redwood era of surfing is almost completely lost due to he difficulty of riding heavy, 10-15 foot long boards. (This decline is reminiscent of the lost art of body surfing—a growth sport in the 1960s, but one in which only a few body surfers excel today.) The Hawaiian heritage dates back centuries to the true spirit of surfing, but few surfers today could ride an "Olo," which was ridden by the chiefs, or an "Alaia," ridden by the commoners. Such boards were 15 feet long, 19 inches wide, and weighed 100 pounds. These hardwood and dark wood boards were made using the wiliwili, the ula, and the koa trees.

Today's modern replicas of early '60s boards are mostly made from balsa wood, which rides lower in the water than foam per cubic foot of material. Traditional balsa board manufacturers are keeping alive a feeling of surfing the "real" way, in hot dog style. When you surf on balsa you come alive to the beauty of lightweight grained wood. It wants to go down the line fast, and no other material can give that feeling. You revisit the bliss of surfing's first big craze—of stomps and turns and head dips. When the waves are glassy offshore with overhead high pumping lines and all your energy is rolled into the take-off and ride on a wave that runs three quarters of a mile in tropical or cool clear re-mote water...it's the ultimate journey. Every split second in your adventure becomes more important and more memorable later on.

Chuck's photos presented here provide a unique "behind-the-scenes" look at the contemporary building and shaping of Chuck Bassett balsa surfboards. They were taken at random stages of the process and show several different boards in production.

All photos in this section are courtesy of Chuck Bassett, Fine Balsa Wood Surfboards.

Balsa wood and hardwood stringer design with paper template; dry set-up.

Planing and inspection of multi-stringer board.

Blank ready to be cut.

Holding the template and drawing the pencil line.

Using a Skil worm-driven saw for the cross-cutting process.

Cutting the template.

Clamping under even pressure.

Laying out the template.

Blank being planed.

Gluing on the hardwood tail block.

Applying pressure.

Rough shape.

Foil-planing the rails.

Planing stringers.

Shaping the rail.

Rolling the rails.

Ready for fine sanding.

Ready to hand-smooth.

Measuring the width.

Hand-planing the stringer.

Clamping in sections.

Checking plan and shaping. Beginning rough shaping using a Skil-100 Planer.

Turning rails using a Skil-100 Planer.

Ready for glassing.

Fine grinding.

Beaded fin, ready to gloss.

Finished fin.

Laying down the fiberglass cloth; cutting and trimming.

Wave shape design.

Fins ready to be glossed.

Cutting out the plan shape from both sides with a Skil-77 saw.

Setting up to glue on the tail block.

Band-sawing.

Clamping the fin; Hawaiian Koa and African Zebra woods used.

If the joint is true, masking tape provides adequate pressure.

Using Honduras mahogany and basswood, the fin is drum-sanded to desired thickness.

Beaded fin mold for the fiberglass edge.

Orbital sander to roughly shape for final sanding.

Cutting out on a band saw.

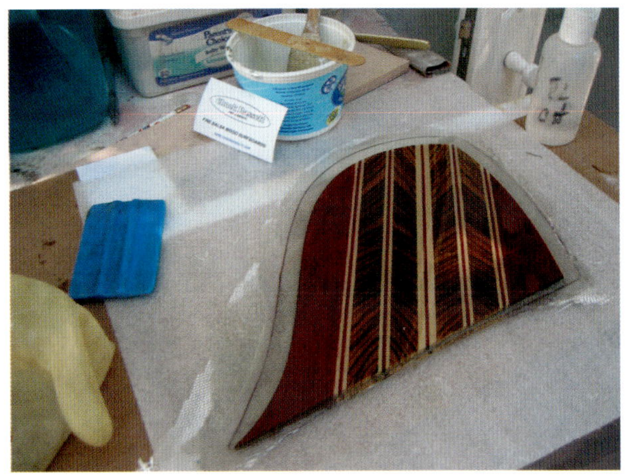

Fin for sanding.

Stringers cut.

A router and band saw are used to cut out each fin segment.

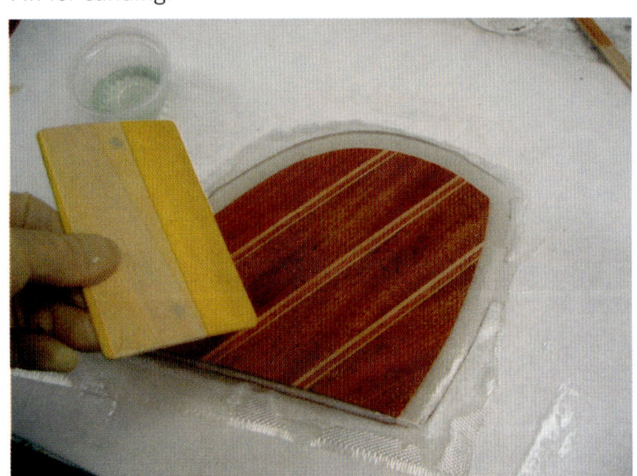

Final glassing.

Template drawn.

Marking out Hot Curl shape.

Chuck Bassett surfboards.

Mango and Zebra wood fins.

Chuck Bassett's decal on a finished board.

Hot Curl finished with high polish.

Ready to place on board.

Display.

Finished fin.

Fin on a completed board.

Banding the rails.

Chuck Bassett with finished board.

Big wave gun.

Display.

Ready to wax.

Display.

Foam and wood.

The finished big wave gun.

The completed Hot Curl at "Woodies on the Pier" in San Clemente.

Close-up of fins.

Chuck Bassett surfboards.

Traditional board and tail block.

Finished board in display rack.

Tail block and fin.

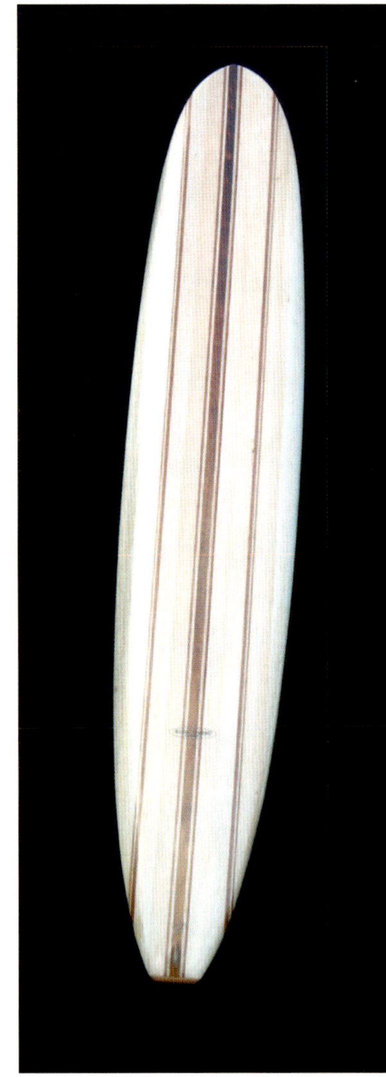

Beauty against a black cloth backdrop.

Buffed and polished, ready for the surf.

Drew Brophy Surfboards

Photo courtesy of Surfboard Art by Drew Brophy.

6’4”, flying fish tail, 2004. $2500.

Photo courtesy of Surfboard Art by Drew Brophy.

6'- 6'9", green room matt, 2005. $6000.

Photo courtesy of Surfboard Art by Drew Brophy.

6'2"- 6'10", nature mural, 2004. $6500.

Pitch Fork

This monster fish is sure to turn some heads in the lineup! With its curved fanged fins, and pitch forked tail, it would be danger to anyone in the water. Drew's Flaming dragon tube leaps out as the surfer lights his way through the tube with a torch. Painted by Drew, Shaped by Gary Wilson of Kinetic Surfboards, Glassed by Todd Sutz.

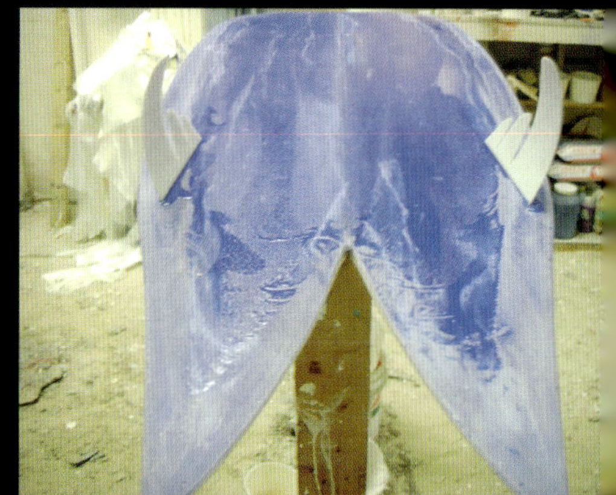

The fanged fins on the glassing rack, ready to be sharpened.

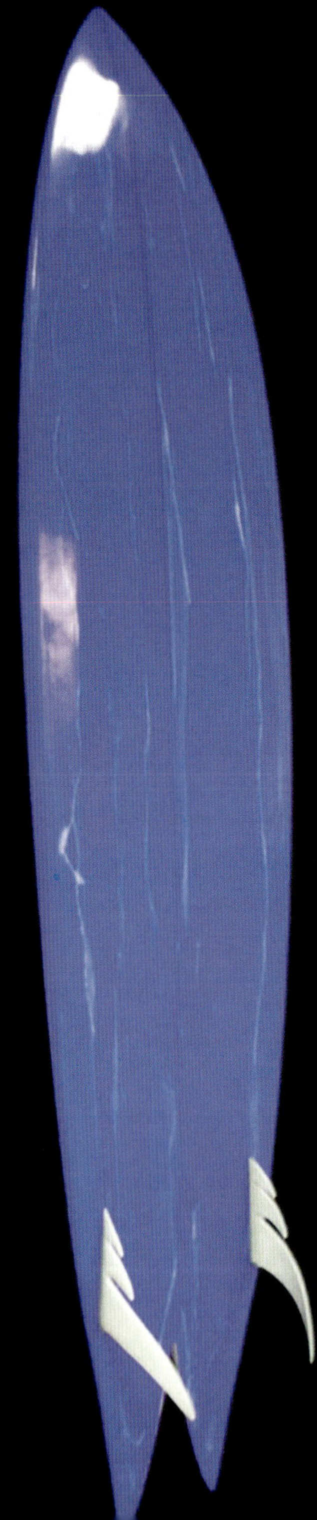

Pitch Fork, 2004. $2000.

Photo courtesy of Surfboard Art by Drew Brophy.

Photo courtesy of Surfboard Art by Drew Brophy.

6'6"-7', Sea World, 2005. $7000.

Photo courtesy of Surfboard Art by Drew Brophy.

8' gun, 2004. $2100.

Photo courtesy of Surfboard Art by Drew Brophy.

8'6", wings, 2005. $3000.

6'8", 2003.
$1200.

Photo courtesy of Surfboard Art by Drew Brophy.

7', wings, 2004.
$2000.

Photo courtesy of Surfboard Art by Drew Brophy.

7'1", winged, 2005.
$3000.

Photo courtesy of Surfboard Art by Drew Brophy.

Photo courtesy of *Surfboard Art* by Drew Brophy.

7', wings bird, 2004. $1800.

Photo courtesy of *Surfboard Art* by Drew Brophy.

7'6", hat, 2005. $2500.

Photo courtesy of *Surfboard Art* by Drew Brophy.

7'6", music, 2004. $1600.

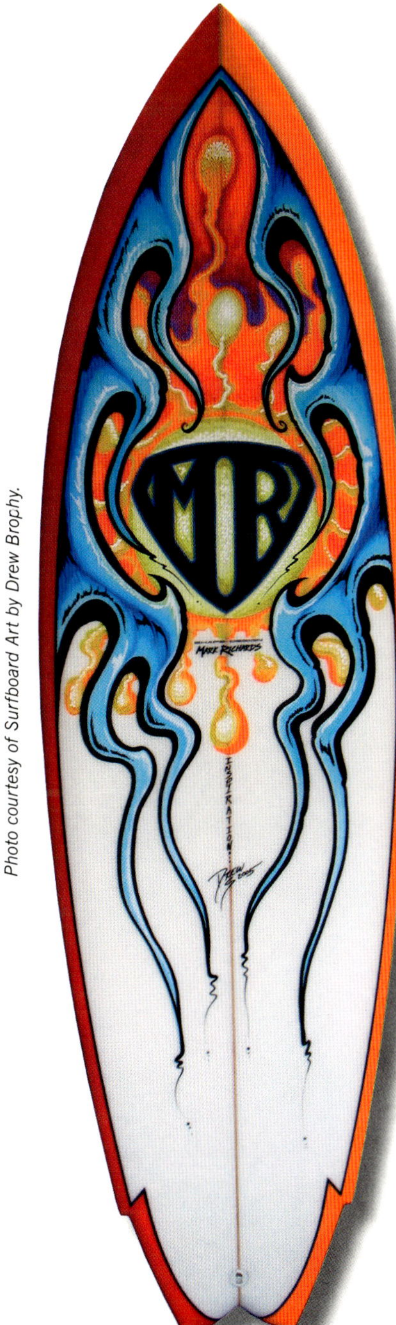

Photo courtesy of *Surfboard Art* by Drew Brophy.

6'10", winged swallow tail, 2004. $2100.

Photo courtesy of Surfboard Art by Drew Brophy.

Photo courtesy of Surfboard Art by Drew Brophy.

Photo courtesy of Surfboard Art by Drew Brophy.

Drew Brophy with a selection of his boards.

6'8", thruster. $2400. Inspired by a surf movie poster of the 1970s.

Photo courtesy of Surfboard Art by Drew Brophy.

Photo courtesy of Surfboard Art by Drew Brophy.

Designs to inspire.

A collection of Drew Brophy's art.

Photo courtesy of Surfboard Art by Drew Brophy.

Off the lip, John Sumpter.

Bunger Surfboards

Photo courtesy of Charlie Bunger, Bunger Surfboards.

Photo courtesy of Charlie Bunger, Bunger Surfboards.

6'4", 2005. $500.

Photo courtesy of Charlie Bunger, Bunger Surfboards.

6'8", 2005. $600.

9'6", 2004. $600.

Photo courtesy of Charlie Bunger, Bunger Surfboards.

9'5", triple stringer, 2002. $1000.

Photo courtesy of Charlie Bunger, Bunger Surfboards.

12" x 12" plaque, 2000. $300.

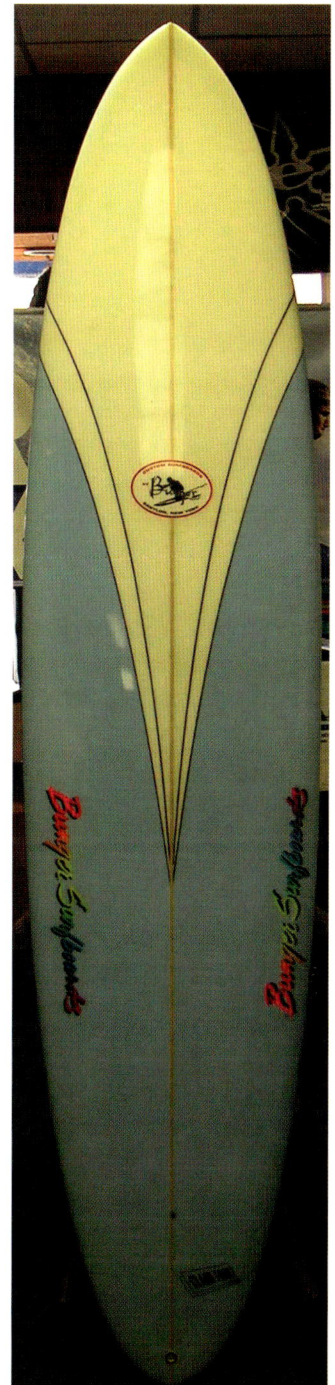

Photo courtesy of Charlie Bunger, Bunger Surfboards.

7'6", 2003. $800.

Photo courtesy of Charlie Bunger, Bunger Surfboards.

9'3", 2004. $600.

Tim Bessell Surfboards

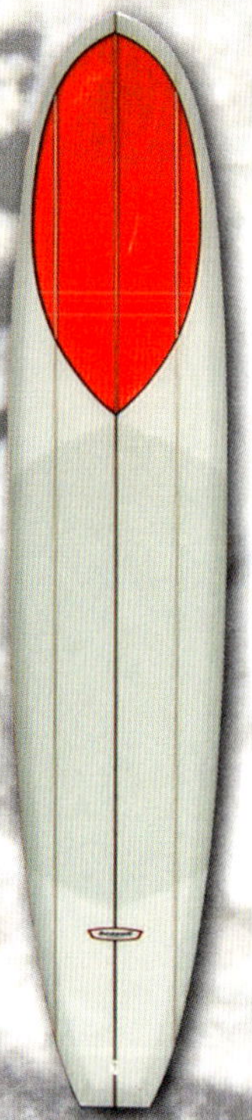

9'6", nose rider, 2005. $1000.

Photo courtesy of Tim Bessell.

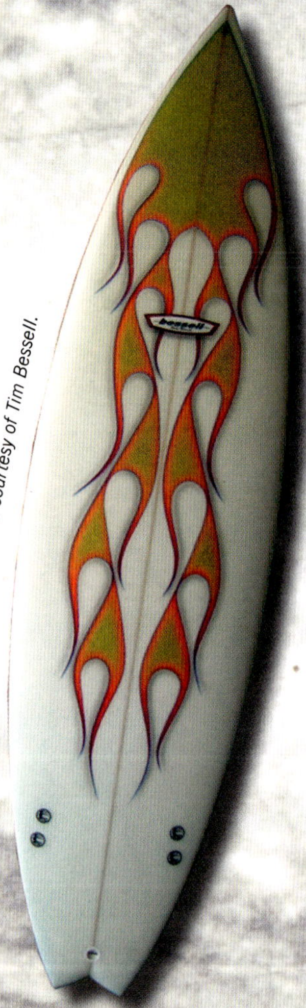

6'6", flames, 2005. $700.

Photo courtesy of Tim Bessell.

9'4", triple stringer, 2005. $1400.

Photo courtesy of Tim Bessell.

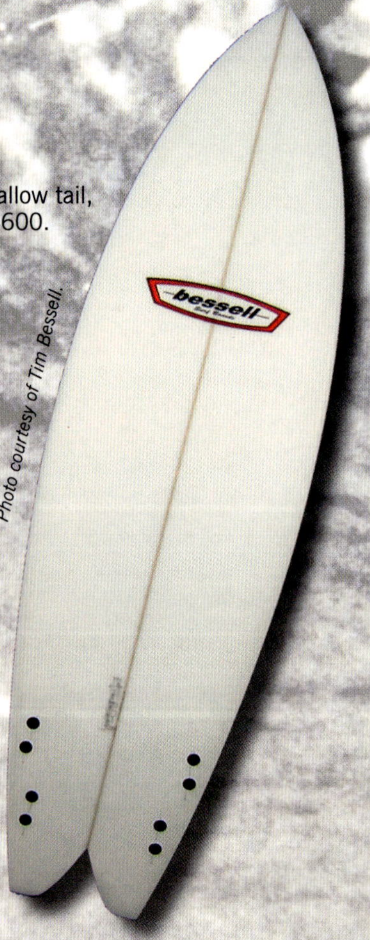

6'3", swallow tail, 2005. $600.

Photo courtesy of Tim Bessell.

Con Surfboards

Photo courtesy of Bruce Grant and Gil Talamantes.

9'6", 2005. $800.

Photo courtesy of Bruce Grant and Gil Talamantes.

10', 2005. $900.

Photo courtesy of Bruce Grant and Gil Talamantes.

9'8", 2005. $1000.

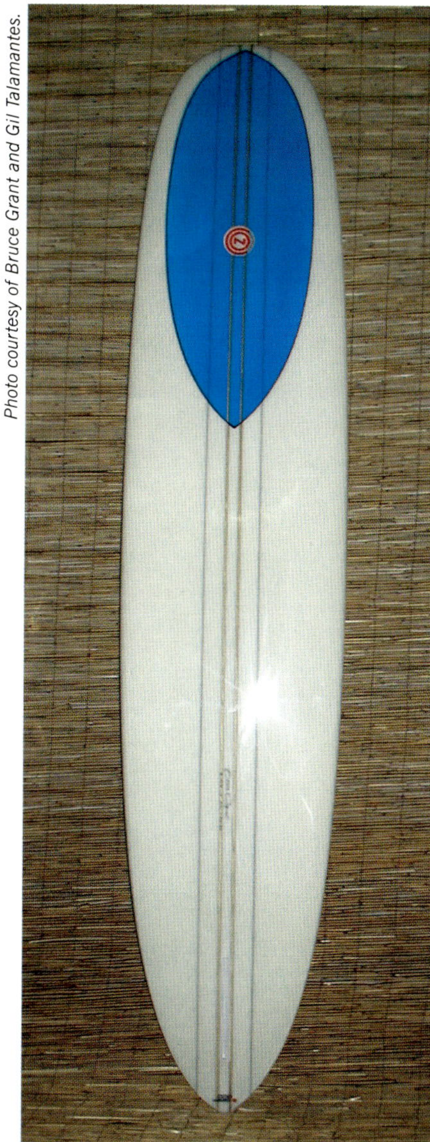

Photo courtesy of Bruce Grant and Gil Talamantes.

9'10", 2005. $1000.

Photo courtesy of Bruce Grant and Gil Talamantes.

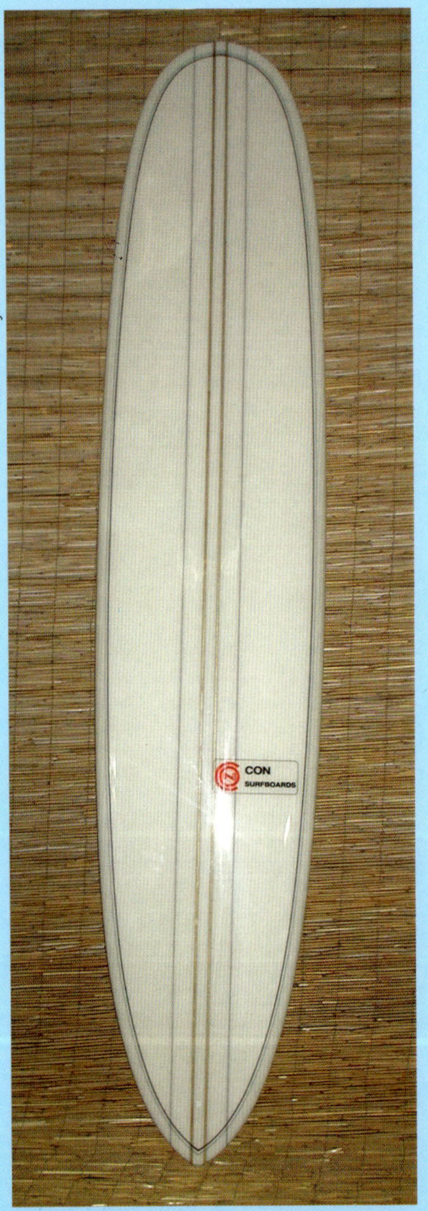

9'4", 2005. $1000.

Photo courtesy of Bruce Grant and Gil Talamantes.

8'6", 2004. $700.

Photo courtesy of Bruce Grant and Gil Talamantes.

7'6", 2005. $500.

Photo courtesy of Bruce Grant and Gil Talamantes.

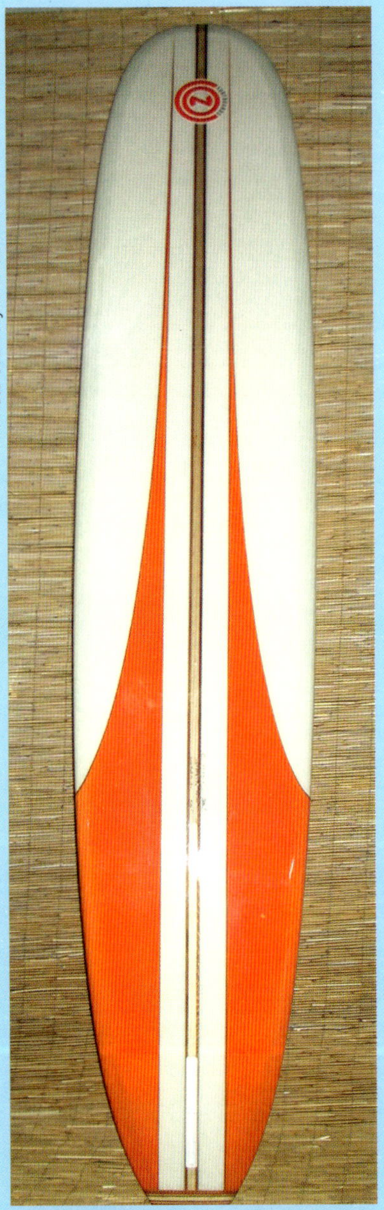

9'6", 2005. $1100.

Photo courtesy of Bruce Grant and Gil Talamantes.

9', 2005. $700.

Photo courtesy of Bruce Grant and Gil Talamantes.

9'10", 2004. $700.

Photo courtesy of Bruce Grant and Gil Talamantes.

9'6", 2005. $1100.

Photo courtesy of Bruce Grant and Gil Talamantes.

8'10", 2005. $600.

Photo courtesy of Bruce Grant and Gil Talamantes.

9'3", 2005. $1000.

Photo courtesy of Bruce Grant and Gil Talamantes.

9'7", 2005. $800.

Photo courtesy of Bruce Grant and Gil Talamantes.

9'6", 2005. $1200.

Photo courtesy of Bruce Grant and Gil Talamantes.

9'8", 2005. $1100.

Photo courtesy of Bruce Grant and Gil Talamantes.

9'8", 2005. $1100.

Photo courtesy of Bruce Grant and Gil Talamantes.

9'3", 2004. $700.

Photo courtesy of Bruce Grant and Gil Talamantes.

9'8", 2005. $800.

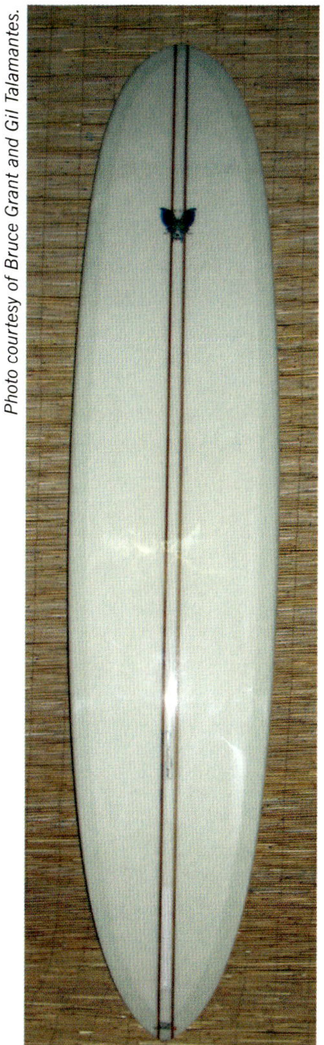

Photo courtesy of Bruce Grant and Gil Talamantes.

9'4", 2004. $800.

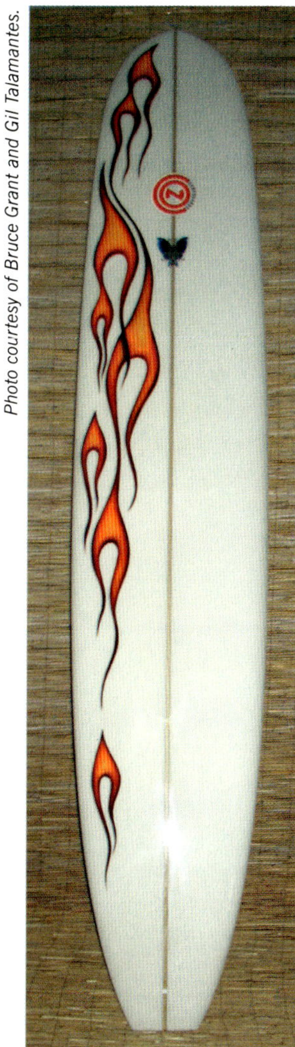

Photo courtesy of Bruce Grant and Gil Talamantes.

10', 2004. $1000.

malibulongboards.com

The photos here show one surfer's private collection of original boards.

Photo courtesy of malibulongboards.com.

9'6", Mal, Bingstock. $2500.

Photo courtesy of malibulongboards.com.

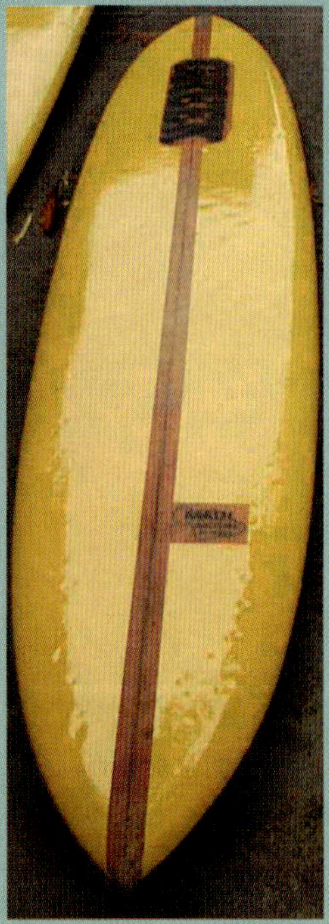

9'8", Mal, Greek. $2000.

Photo courtesy of malibulongboards.com.

10', Greg Noll. $4000.

Photo courtesy of malibulongboards.com.

8'6", Hannon. $700.

Photo courtesy of malibulongboards.com.

9'6", Hobie. $2000.

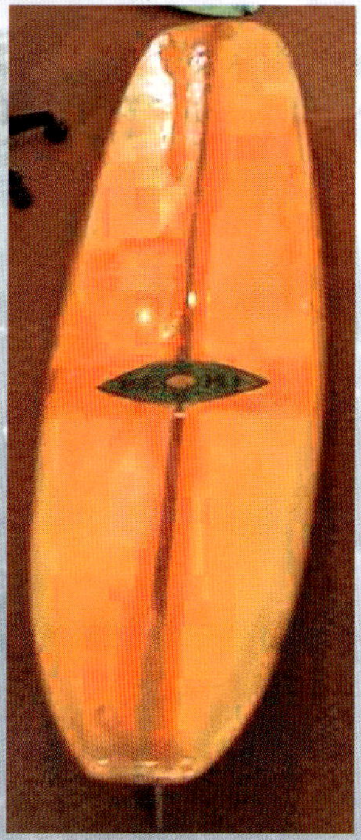

Photo courtesy of malibulongboards.com.

9'8", Keoki. $700.

Photo courtesy of malibulongboards.com.

9'10", Liddle. $1500.

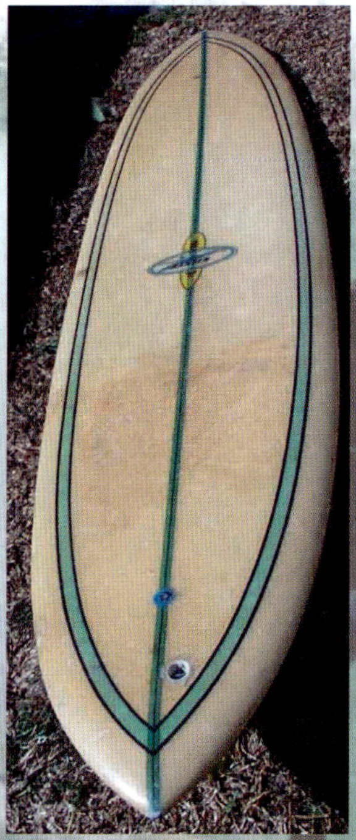

Photo courtesy of malibulongboards.com.

9'2", Mike Doyle. $1700.

Photo courtesy of malibulongboards.com.

10', poput2. $400.

Photo courtesy of malibulongboards.com.

7'2", rbbolt. $2200.

8', rickvee. $600.

9'6", Sweetdeck. $700.

7'6", Robert. $1500.

9'8", Wardy. $2400.

Hobie Surfboards

Photo by kind permission of Seabase Ltd.

6'4" fish tail, 2005. $500.

Photo by kind permission of Seabase Ltd.

6' fish tail, 2005. $500.

Photo by kind permission of Seabase Ltd.

6'2" fish tail, 2005. $500.

Photo by kind permission of Seabase Ltd.

6'6", square tail, 2004. $500.

Photo by kind permission of Seabase Ltd.

6'1" fish tail, 2005. $500.

Photo by kind permission of Seabase Ltd.

6'5" fish tail, 2005. $500.

Photo by kind permission of Seabase Ltd.

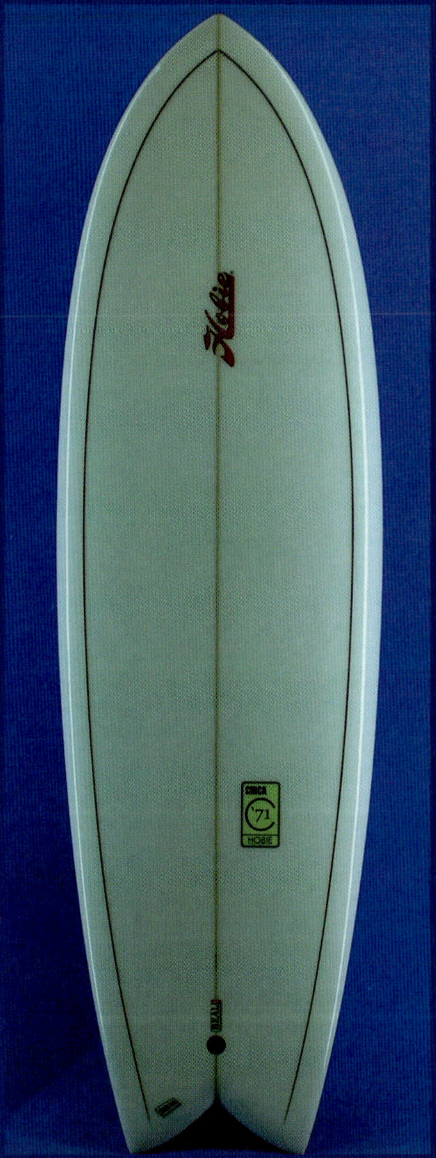

6'6" fish tail, 2005. $400.

Photo by kind permission of Seabase Ltd.

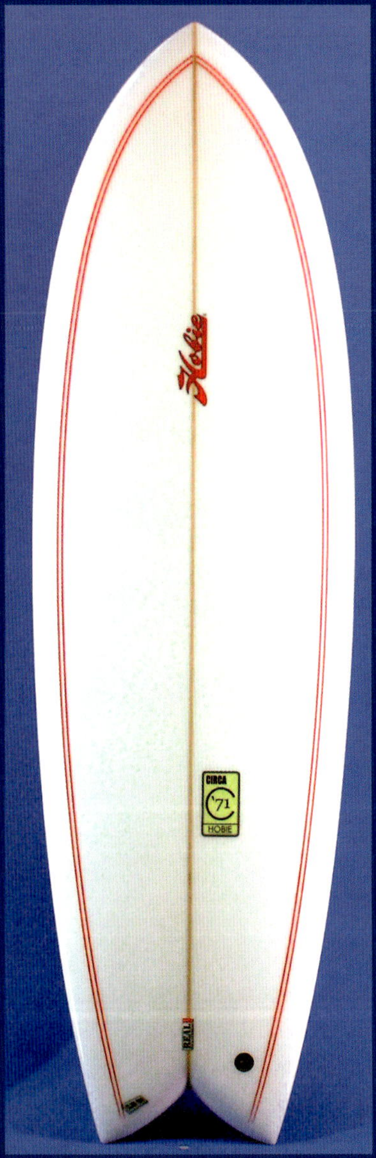

6'1" fish tail, 2005. $500.

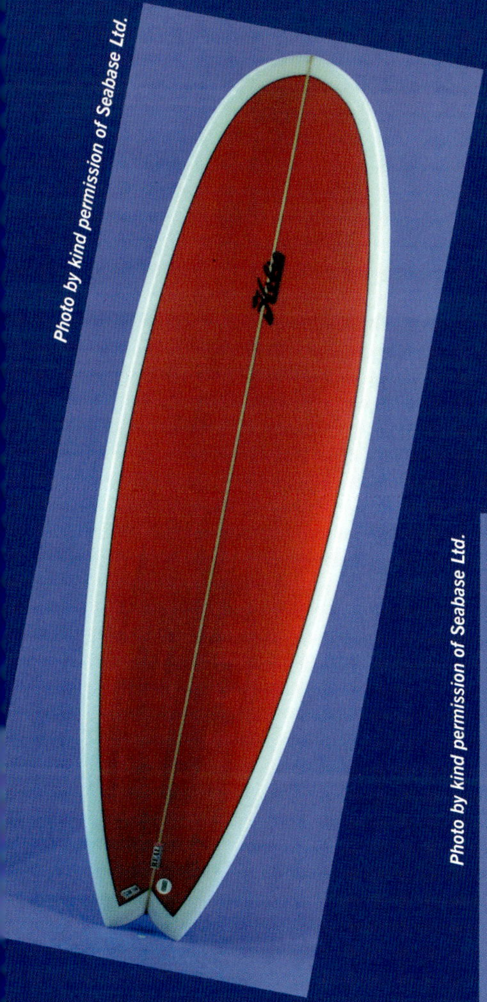

Photo by kind permission of Seabase Ltd.

6'1" swallow tail, 2005. $500.

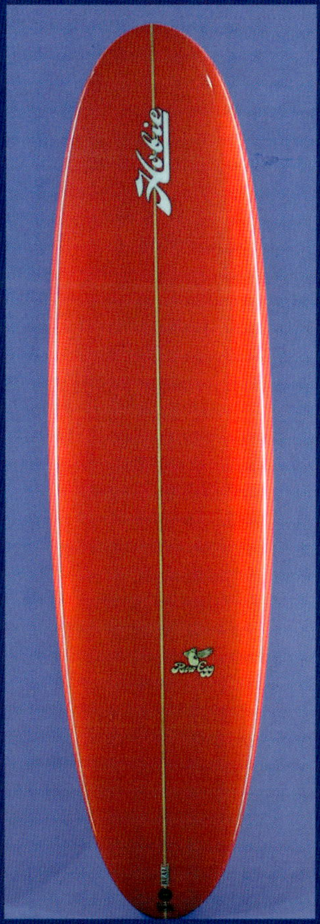

Photo by kind permission of Seabase Ltd.

6'1", round tail, 2005. $600.

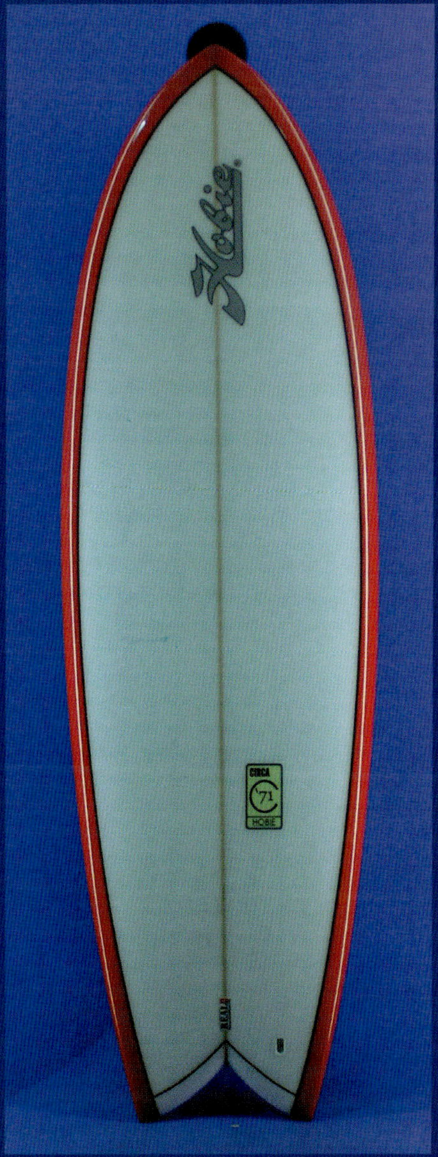

Photo by kind permission of Seabase Ltd.

6'2", fish tail, 2005. $800.

Photo by kind permission of Seabase Ltd.

9'1", Mal, 2005. $800.

Photo by kind permission of Seabase Ltd.

9'4", Mal, 2005. $500.

Photo by kind permission of Seabase Ltd.

7', Min mal, round tail, 2005. $600.

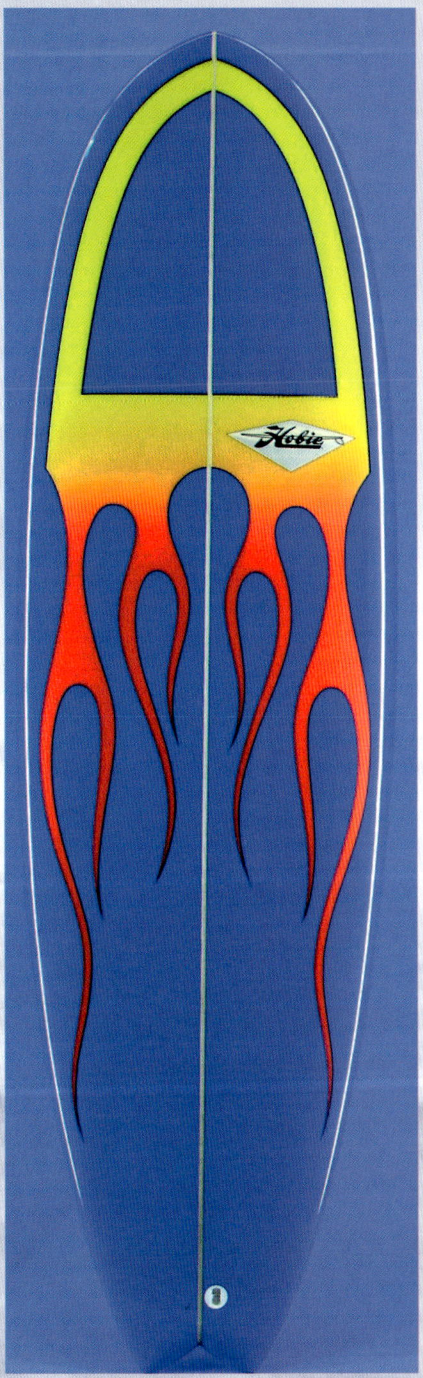

6'1", swallow tail, 2005. $800.

Photo by kind permission of Seabase Ltd.

6'6", round tail, 2005. $500.

Photo by kind permission of Seabase Ltd.

6'1", round tail, 2005. $500.

Photo by kind permission of Seabase Ltd.

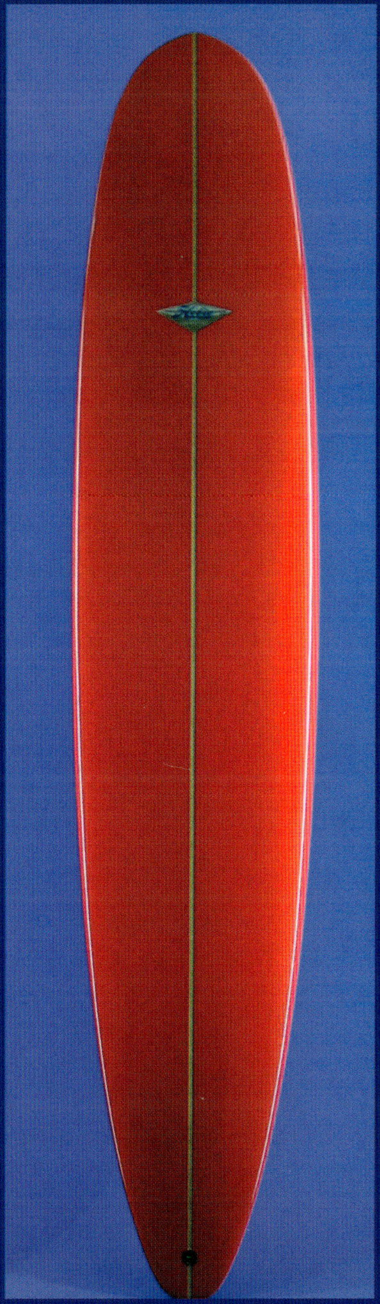

9'6", Mal, square tail, 2005. $1000.

Photo by kind permission of Seabase Ltd.

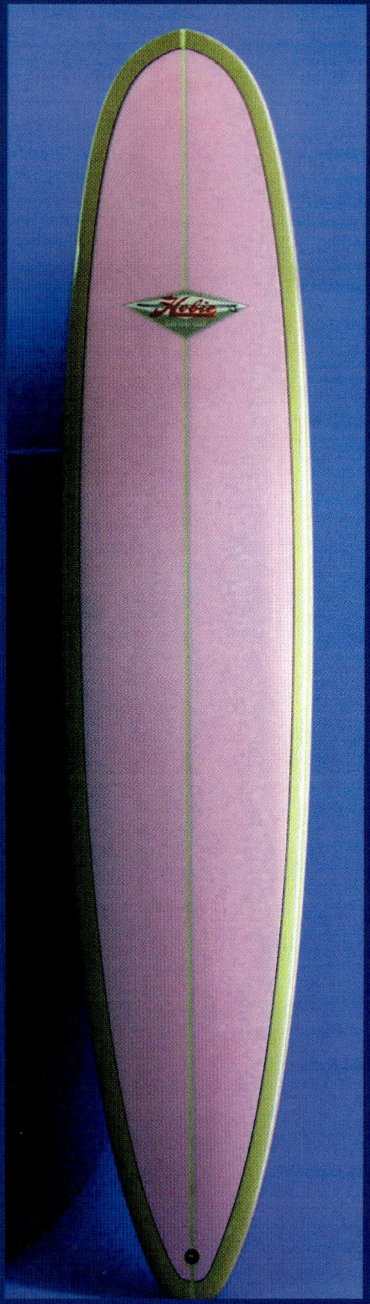

9'6", Mal, squared pin tail, 2005. $1100.

Photo by kind permission of Seabase Ltd.

6'1" round tail,
2005. $500.

Photo by kind permission of Seabase Ltd.

7'1", round tail,
2005. $500.

Photo by kind permission of Seabase Ltd.

6'8", round tail,
2005. $500.

Photo by kind permission of Seabase Ltd.

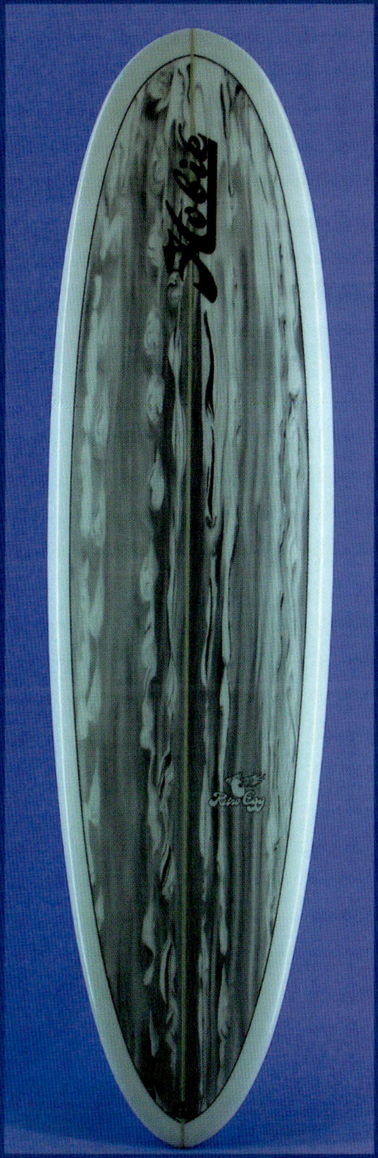

6’1”, round tail, 2005. $500.

Photo by kind permission of Seabase Ltd.

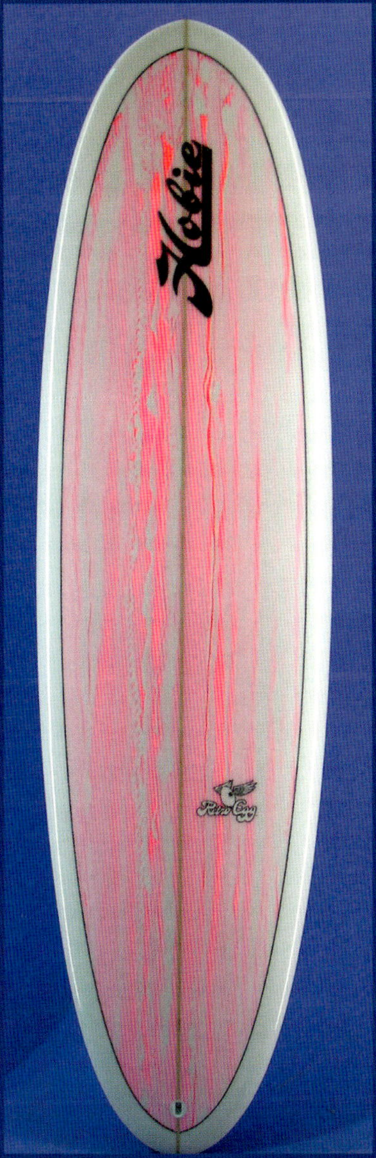

6’4”, round tail, 2005. $500.

Photo by kind permission of Seabase Ltd.

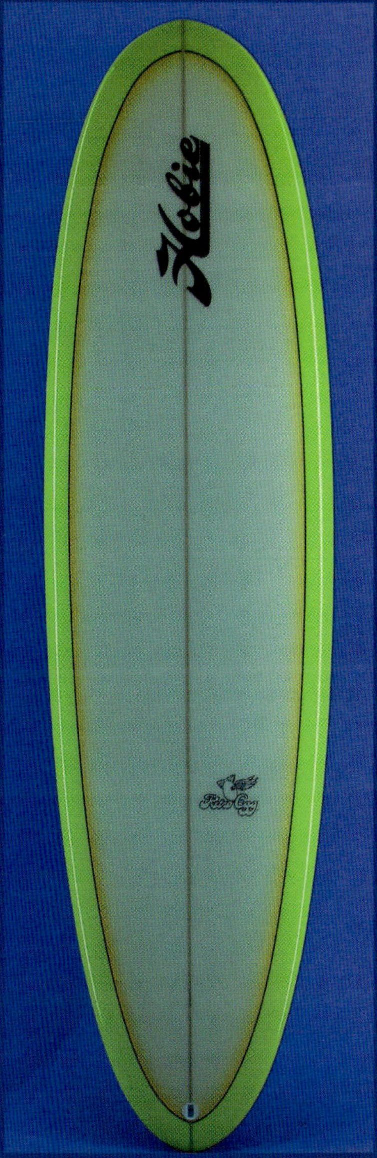

6’0”, round tail, 2005. $500.

Photo by kind permission of Seabase Ltd.

7’5”, round tail, 2005. $700.

7'2", mini mal, round tail, 2005. $500.

Photo by kind permission of Seabase Ltd.

Photo by kind permission of Seabase Ltd.

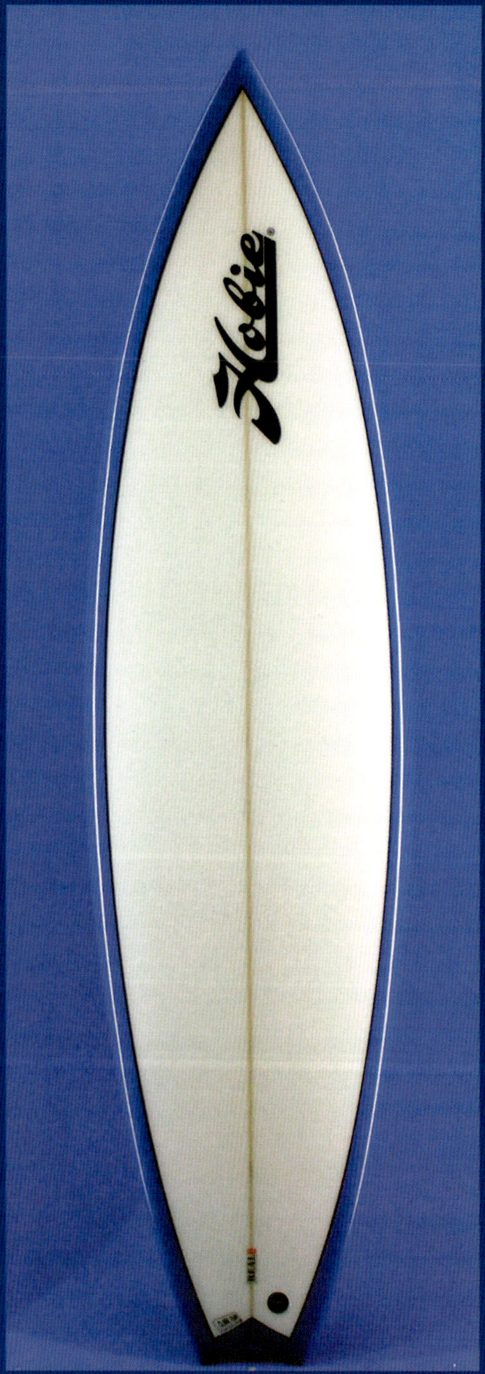

6'1", 2005. $400.

6'3", round tail, 2005. $500.

Photo by kind permission of Seabase Ltd.

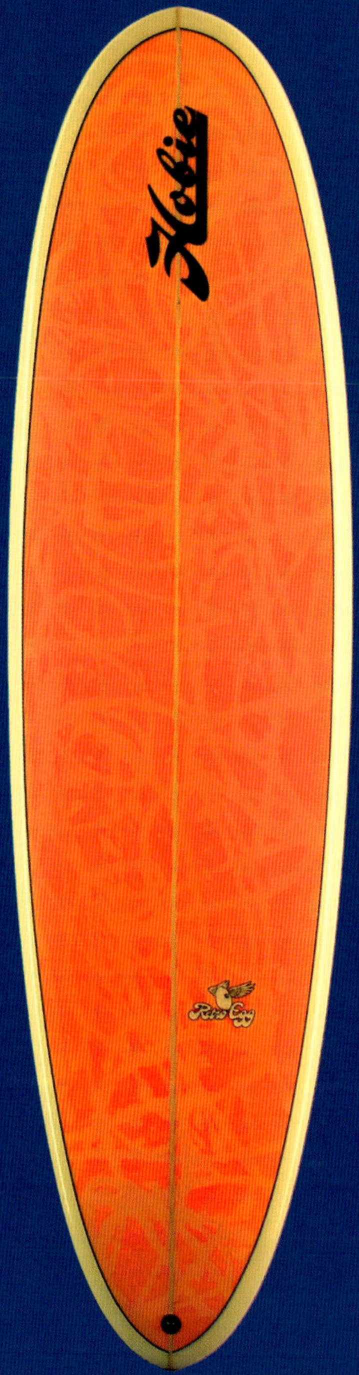

Photo by kind permission of Seabase Ltd.

6'1" fish tail, 2005. $500.

Photo by kind permission of Seabase Ltd.

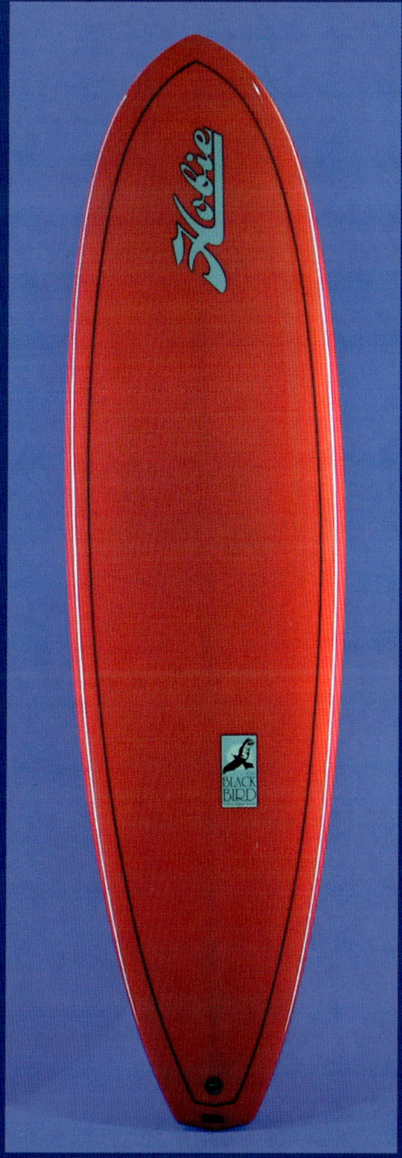

6'8", square tail, 2005. $800.

Photo by kind permission of Seabase Ltd.

6'1" fish tail, 2005. $500.

Photo by kind permission of Seabase Ltd.

6'4" fish tail, 2005. $500.

Photo by kind permission of Seabase Ltd.

6'2" fish tail, 2005. $500.

Photo by kind permission of Seabase Ltd.

6'4", round tail, 2005. $600.

Photo by kind permission of Seabase Ltd.

6'6", round tail, 2005. $500.

Photo by kind permission of Seabase Ltd.

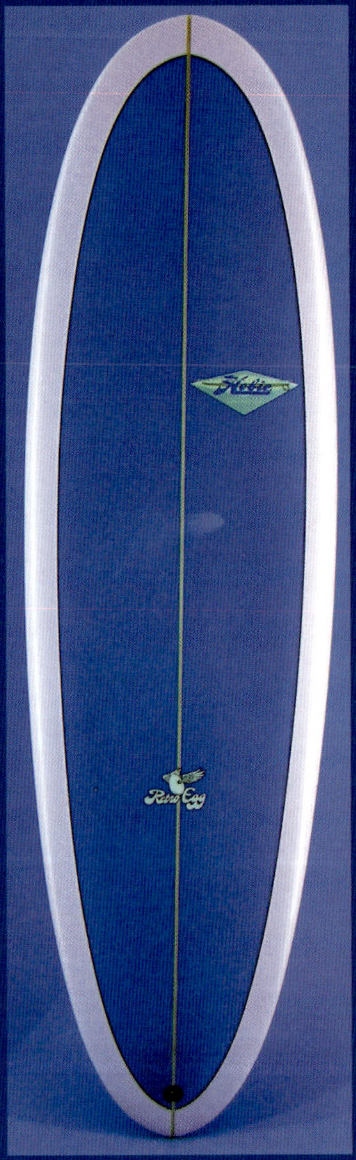

6'0", round tail, 2005. $600.

Photo by kind permission of Seabase Ltd.

6'3", round tail, 2005. $600.

Photo by kind permission of Seabase Ltd.

6'8", round tail, 2005. $600.

Photo by kind permission of Seabase Ltd.

6'5", round tail, 2005. $600.

Photo by kind permission of Seabase Ltd.

6'3", swallow tail, 2005. $600.

Photo by kind permission of Seabase Ltd.

6'6", swallow tail, 2005. $700.

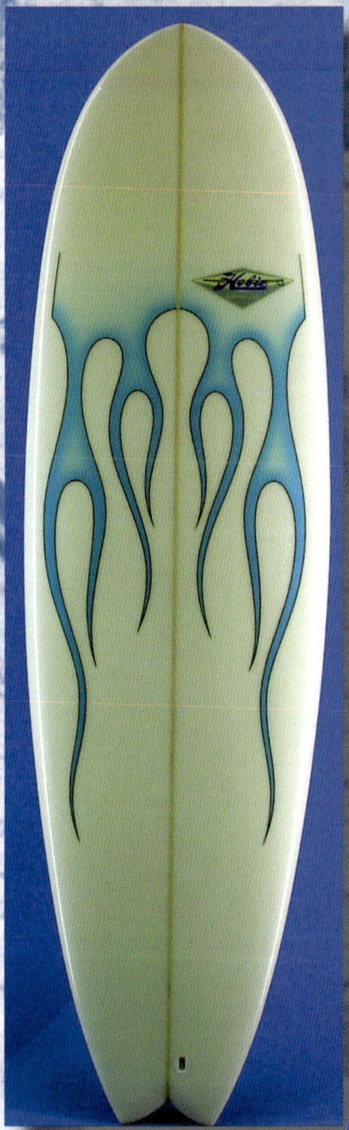

Photo by kind permission of Seabase Ltd.

6'6", swallow tail, 2005. $600.

Photo by kind permission of Seabase Ltd.

6'4", swallow tail, 2005. $1000.

Photo by kind permission of Seabase Ltd.

9'8", Mal, 2005. $1000.

Photo by kind permission of Seabase Ltd.

9'6", round tail, 2005. $600.

Photo by kind permission of Seabase Ltd.

8'10", mini mal, 2005. $1000.

Photo by kind permission of Seabase Ltd.

9'5", Mal, round tail, 2005. $600.

Photo by kind permission of Seabase Ltd.

6'4", round tail, 2005. $600.

Photo by kind permission of Seabase Ltd.

6'4", round tail, 2005. $600.

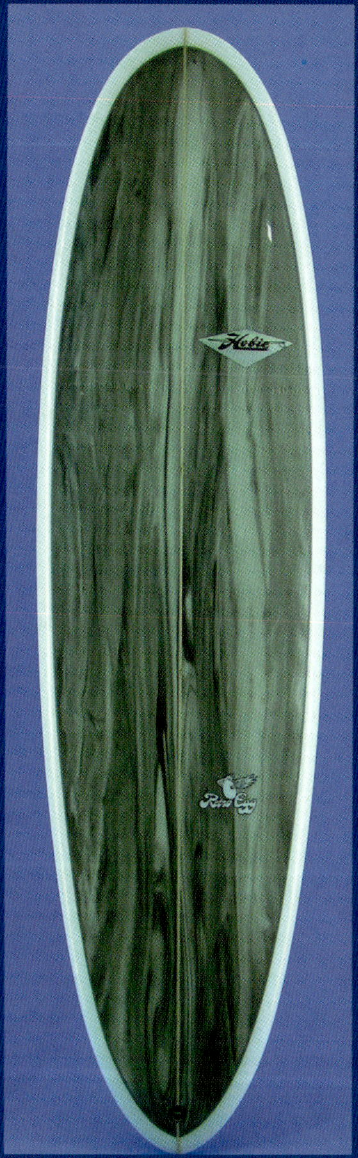

Photo by kind permission of Seabase Ltd.

6'4", round tail, 2005. $600.

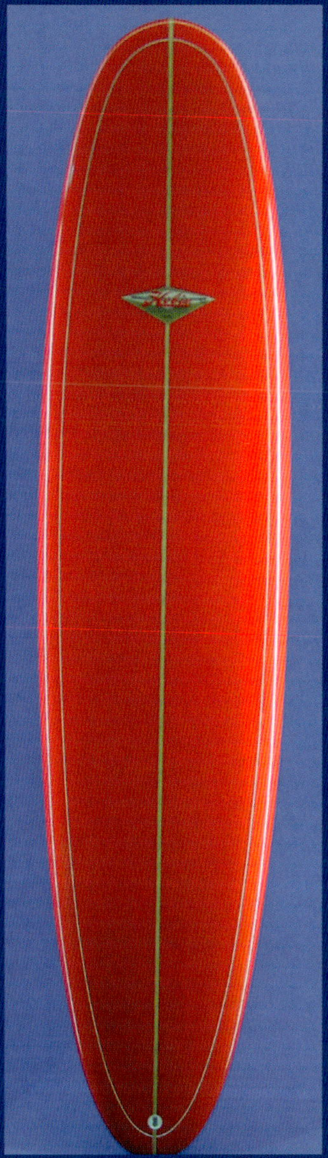

Photo by kind permission of Seabase Ltd.

9'8", Mal, nose rider, 2005. $1100.

Photo by kind permission of Seabase Ltd.

6'2", round tail, 2005. $600.

Photo by kind permission of Seabase Ltd.

6'4", round tail, 2005. $600.

Photo by kind permission of Seabase Ltd.

6'7", round tail, 2005. $600.

Photo by kind permission of Seabase Ltd.

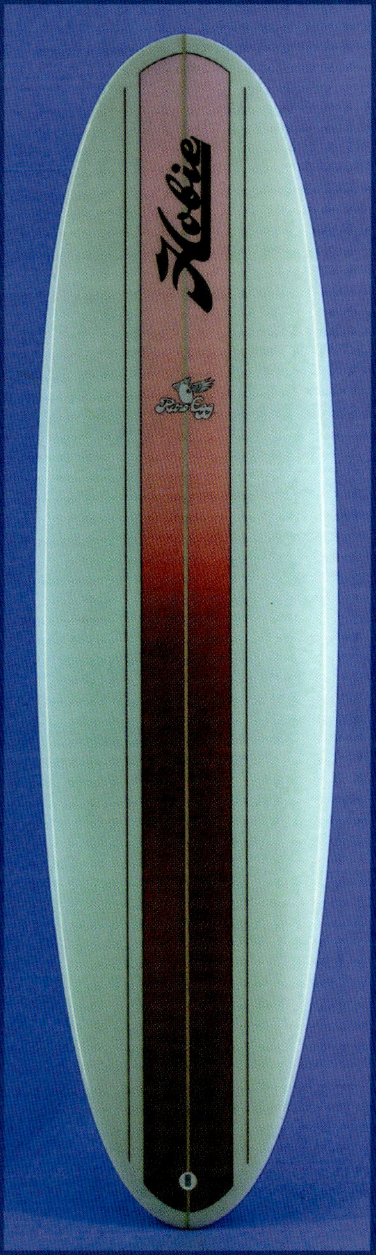

6'5", round tail, 2005. $600.

Photo by kind permission of Seabase Ltd.

6'3", round tail, 2005. $500.

Photo by kind permission of Seabase Ltd.

6'6", round tail, 2005. $500.

Photo by kind permission of Seabase Ltd.

6'4", round tail, 2005. $600.

Photo by kind permission of Seabase Ltd.

6'5", round tail, 2005. $600.

Photo by kind permission of Seabase Ltd.

6'4", round tail, 2005. $600.

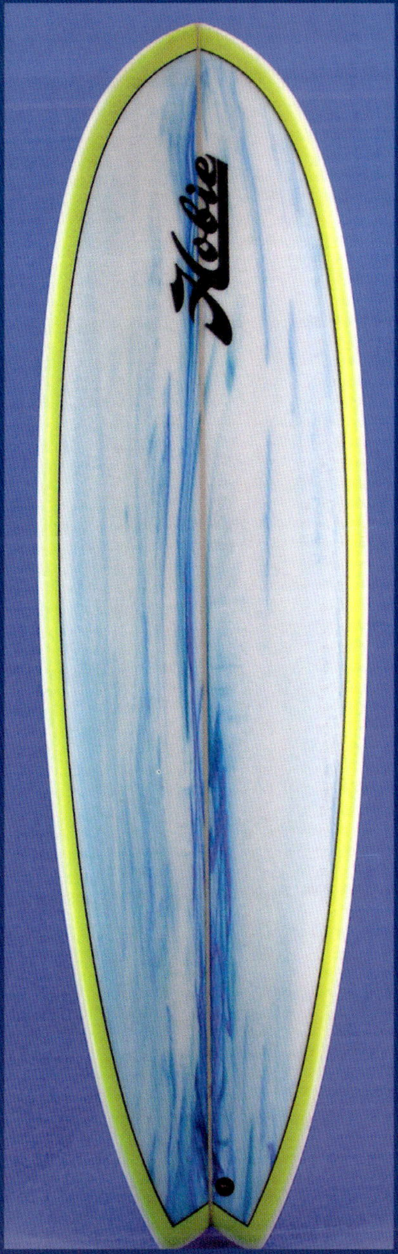

Photo by kind permission of Seabase Ltd.

6'4", swallow tail, 2005. $600.

Photo by kind permission of Seabase Ltd.

6'5", round tail, 2005. $600.

Photo by kind permission of Seabase Ltd.

6'4", round tail, 2005. $600.

Photo by kind permission of Seabase Ltd.

6'4", round tail, 2005. $600.

Photo by kind permission of Seabase Ltd.

6'6", fish tail, 2005. $600.

Photo by kind permission of Seabase Ltd.

7'4", round tail, 2005. $800.

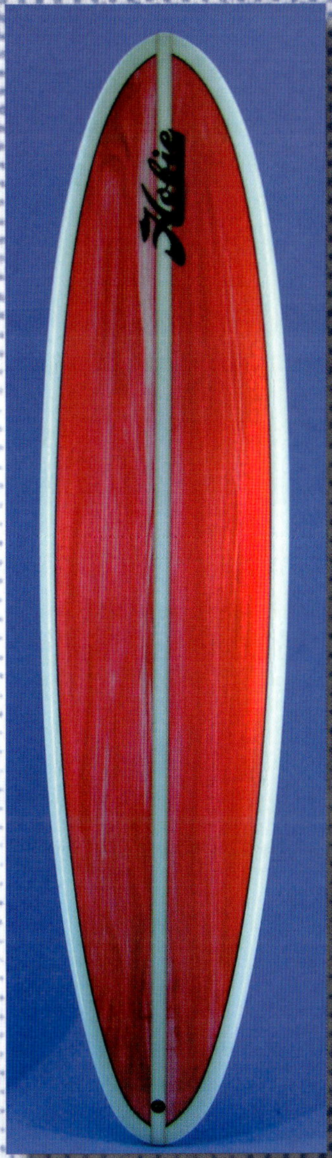

Photo by kind permission of Seabase Ltd.

7'4", round tail, 2005. $800.

Photo by kind permission of Seabase Ltd.

7'4", round tail, 2005. $800.

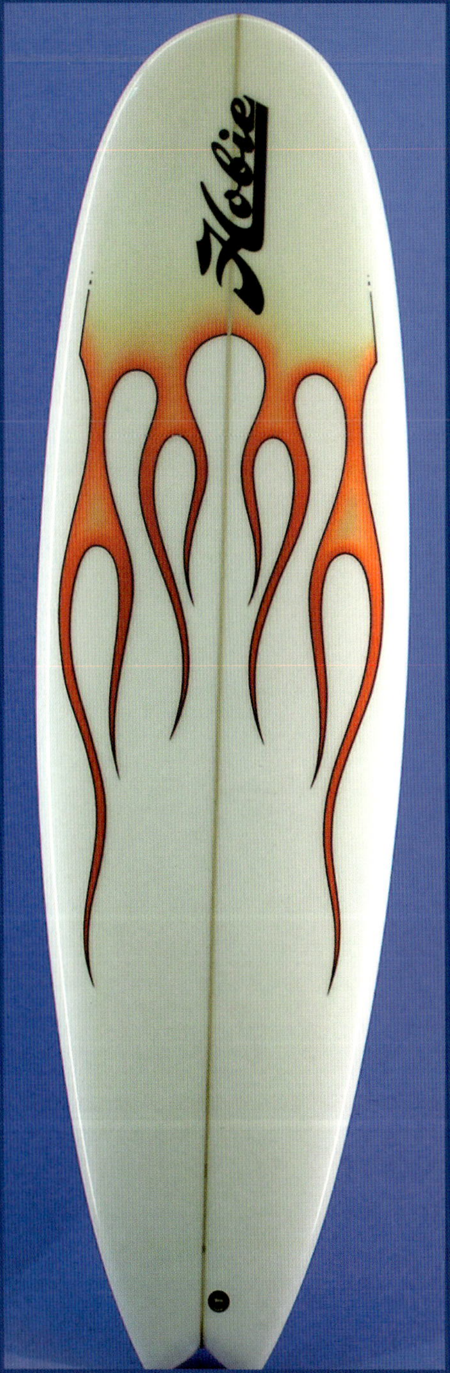

Photo by kind permission of Seabase Ltd.

6'6", swallow tail, 2005. $700.

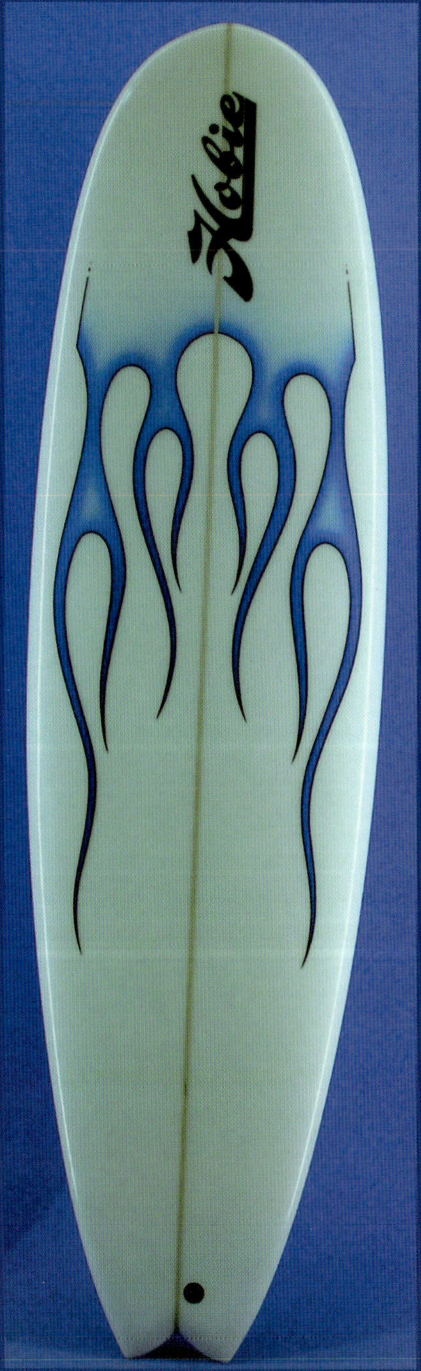

Photo by kind permission of Seabase Ltd.

6'6", swallow tail, 2005. $700.

Photo by kind permission of Seabase Ltd.

6'4", swallow tail, 2005. $600.

Photo by kind permission of Seabase Ltd.

6'4", swallow tail, 2005. $600.

Photo by kind permission of Seabase Ltd.

6'8", round tail, 2005. $600.

Photo by kind permission of Seabase Ltd.

9'4", nose rider, 2005. $1100.

Photo by kind permission of Seabase Ltd.

9'4", Mal, 2005. $1000.

Photo by kind permission of Seabase Ltd.

9'6", Mal, 2005. $900.

Photo by kind permission of Seabase Ltd.

9'4", triple stringer, 2005. $1700.

Photo by kind permission of Seabase Ltd.

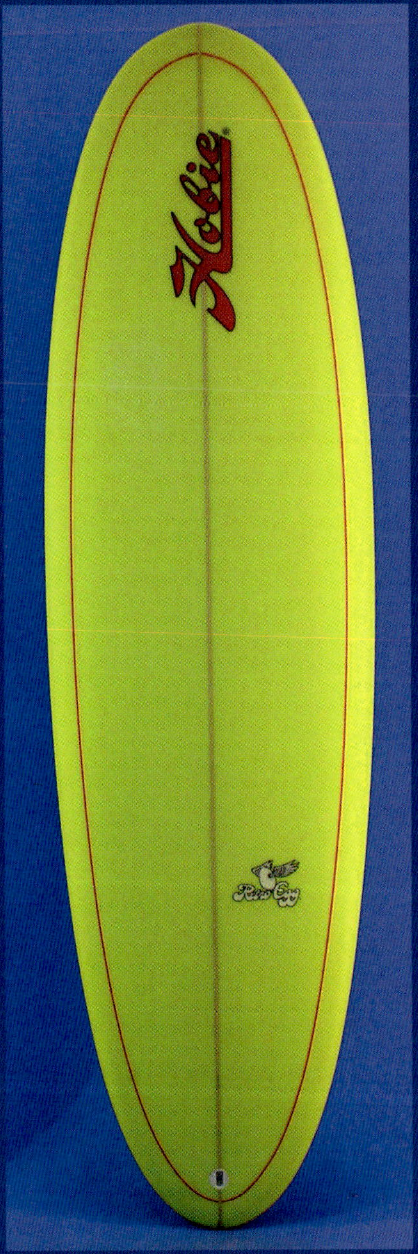

6'4", round tail, 2005. $600.

Photo by kind permission of Seabase Ltd.

6'5", round tail, 2005. $500.

Photo by kind permission of Seabase Ltd.

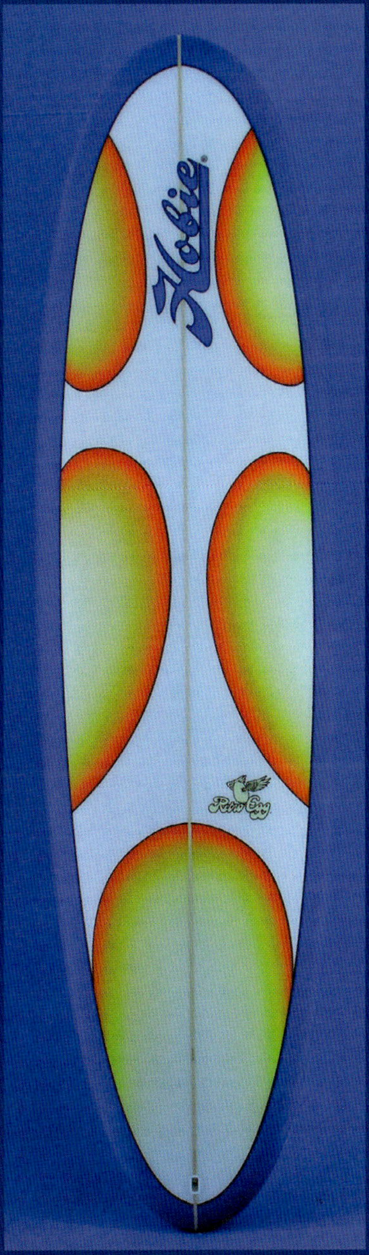

6'8", round tail, 2005. $800.

Photo by kind permission of Seabase Ltd.

6'4", round tail, 2005. $600.

Photo by kind permission of Seabase Ltd.

6'6", round tail, 2005. $700.

Photo by kind permission of Seabase Ltd.

6'5", round tail, 2005. $600.

Photo by kind permission of Seabase Ltd.

6'7", round tail, 2005. $600.

Photo by kind permission of Seabase Ltd.

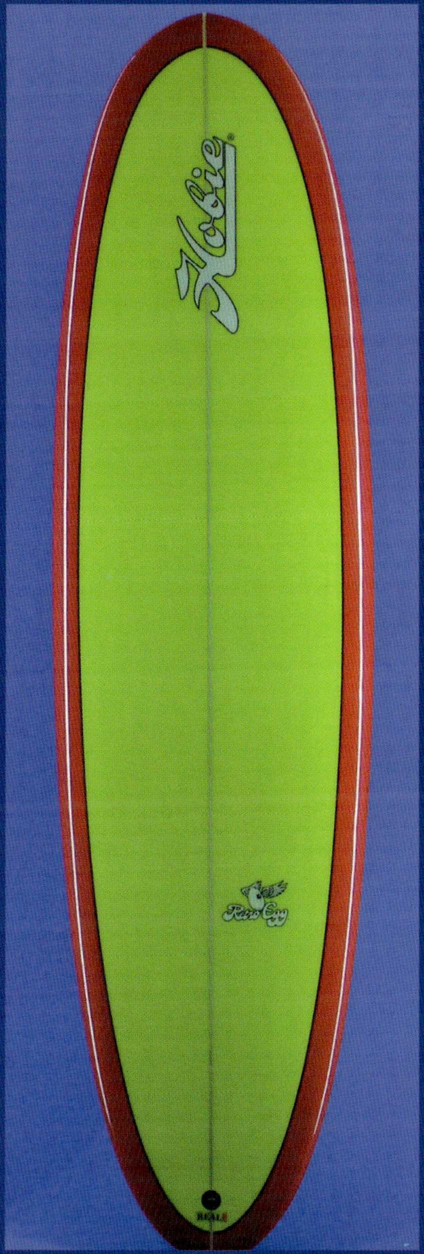

6'6", round tail, 2005. $600.

Photo by kind permission of Seabase Ltd.

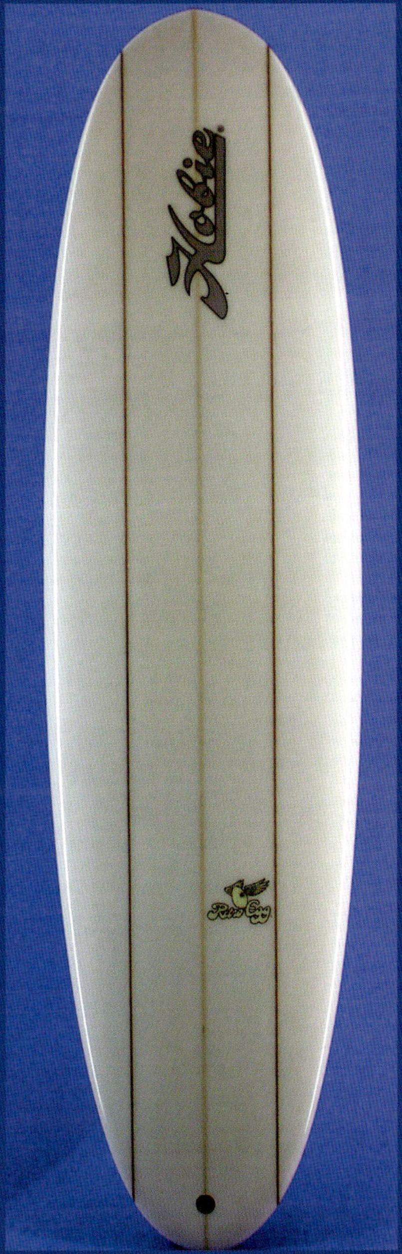

6'3", triple stringer, 2005. $1000.

Photo by kind permission of Seabase Ltd.

6'5", round tail, 2005. $600.

Photo by kind permission of Seabase Ltd.

6'8", triple stringer, 2005. $1000.

Photo by kind permission of Seabase Ltd.

6'4", round tail, 2005. $600.

Photo by kind permission of Seabase Ltd.

9'8", Mal, 2005. $1000.

Photo by kind permission of Seabase Ltd.

6'4", round tail, 2005. $600.

Photo by kind permission of Seabase Ltd.

6'6" fish tail, 2005. $600.

Photo by kind permission of Seabase Ltd.

9'8", Mal, 2005. $1000.

Photo by kind permission of Seabase Ltd.

6'4" fish tail, 2005. $500.

Photo by kind permission of Seabase Ltd.

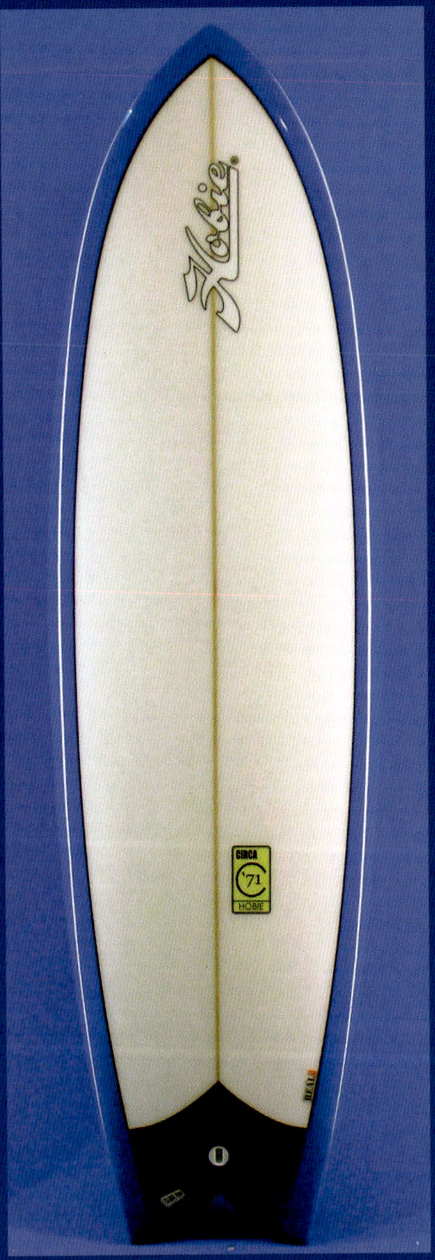

6'4" fish tail, 2005. $600.

Photo by kind permission of Seabase Ltd.

6'6", square tail, 2005. $600.

Photo by kind permission of Seabase Ltd.

6'4", square tail, 2005. $600.

Photo by kind permission of Seabase Ltd.

6'1", square tail, 2005. $600.

Photo by kind permission of Seabase Ltd.

6'4", swallow tail, 2005. $600.

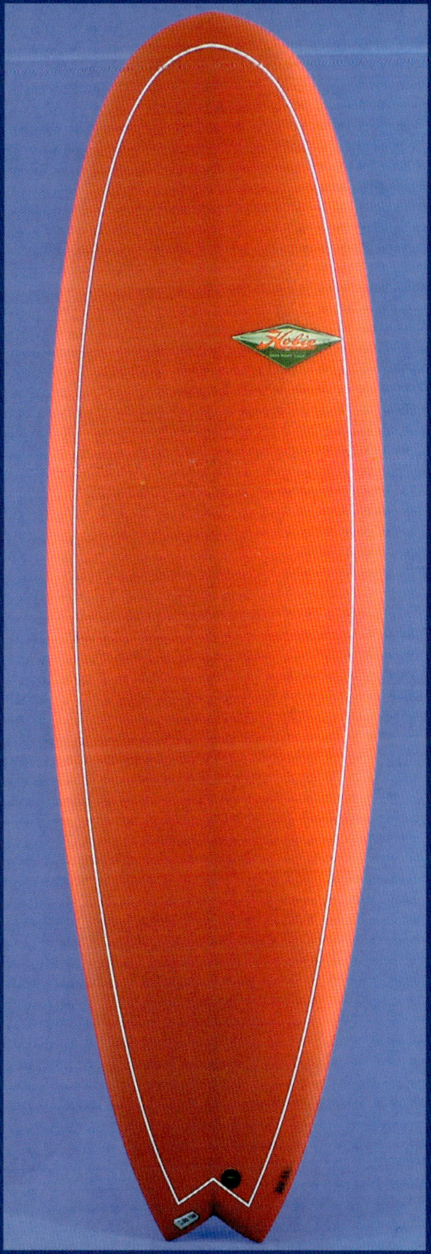

Photo by kind permission of Seabase Ltd.

6'6", swallow tail, 2005. $700.

Photo by kind permission of Seabase Ltd.

6'4", swallow tail, 2005. $600.

6'0", swallow tail, 2005. $600.

Photo by kind permission of Seabase Ltd.

Photo by kind permission of Seabase Ltd.

6'4", swallow tail, 2005. $600.

Photo by kind permission of Seabase Ltd.

6'6", fish tail, 2005. $600.

Photo by kind permission of Seabase Ltd.

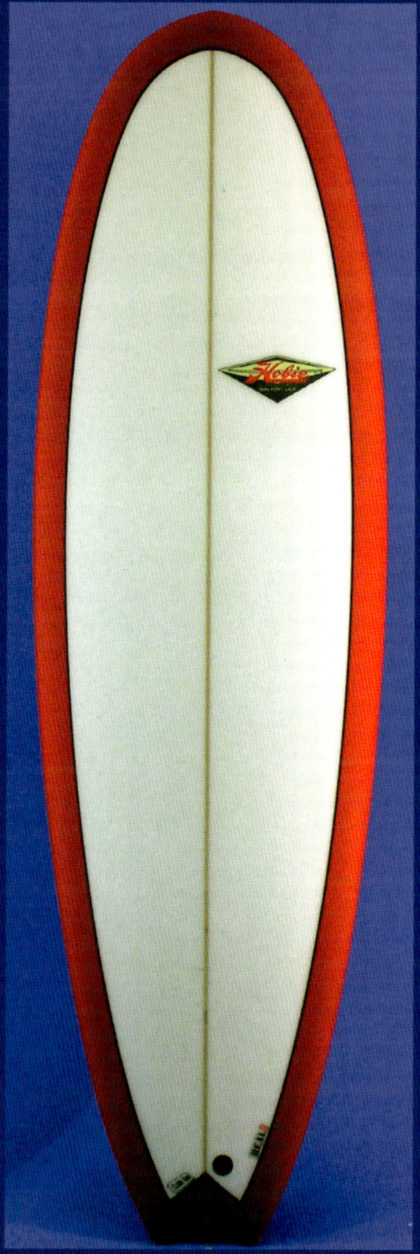

6'5", swallow tail, 2005. $500.

Photo by kind permission of Seabase Ltd.

6'7", swallow tail, 2005. $600.

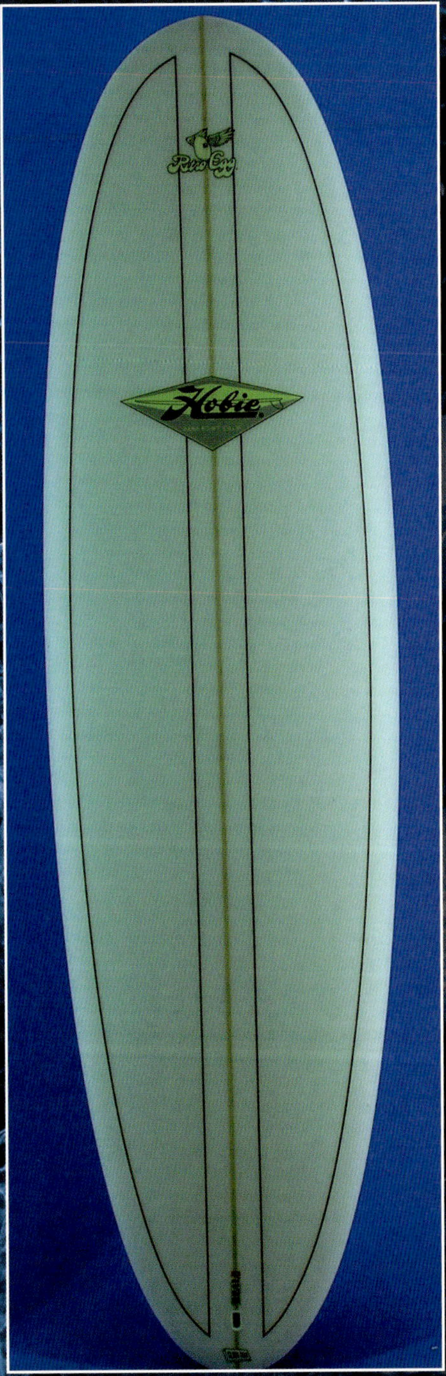

Photo by kind permission of Seabase Ltd.

6'4", round tail, 2005. $600.

10'0", Mal, 2005. $1200.

Photo by kind permission of Seabase Ltd.

Going surfing.

Stewart Surfboards

Photo by kind permission of Seabase Ltd.

9'1", 2005.
$900.

Photo by kind permission of Seabase Ltd.

6'4", 2005.
$500.

Photo by kind permission of Seabase Ltd.

6'2", 2005.
$600.

Photo by kind permission of Seabase Ltd.

6'10", 2004. $600.

Photo by kind permission of Seabase Ltd.

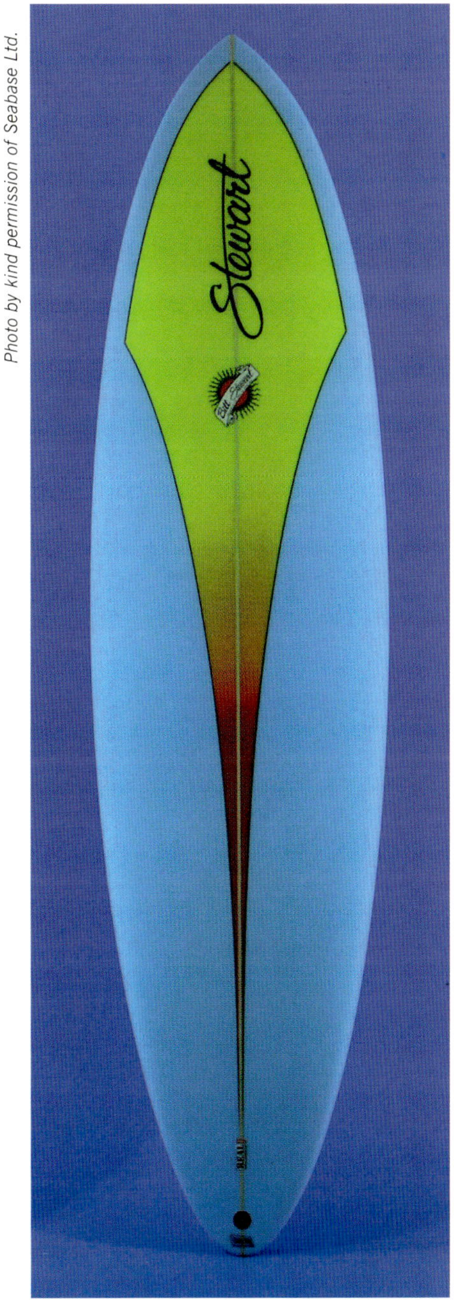

6'6", 2005. $600.

Photo by kind permission of Seabase Ltd.

6'4" fish tail, 2005. $600.

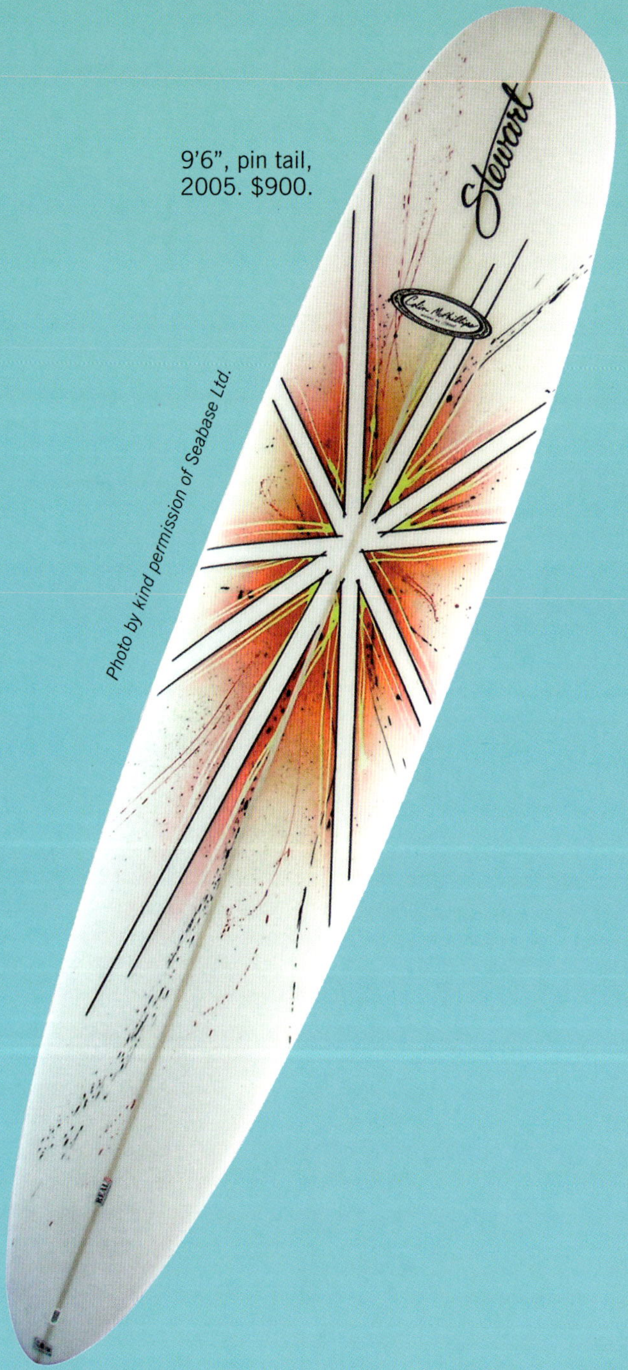

9'6", pin tail, 2005. $900.

Photo by kind permission of Seabase Ltd.

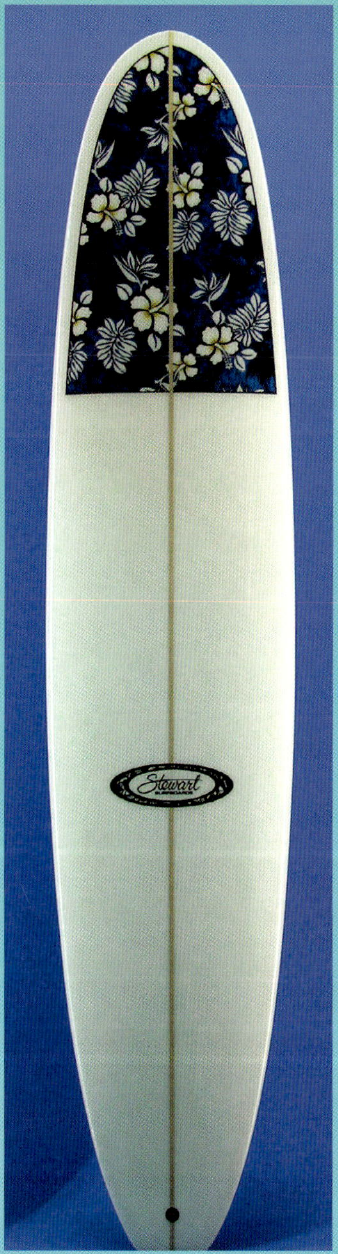

Photo by kind permission of Seabase Ltd.

9'4", Mal, nose rider, 2005. $1000.

Photo by kind permission of Seabase Ltd.

10', Mal, 2005. $1000.

Photo by kind permission of Seabase Ltd.

9'8", Mal, 2005. $900.

Photo by kind permission of Seabase Ltd.

6'7", swallow tail, 2005. $600.

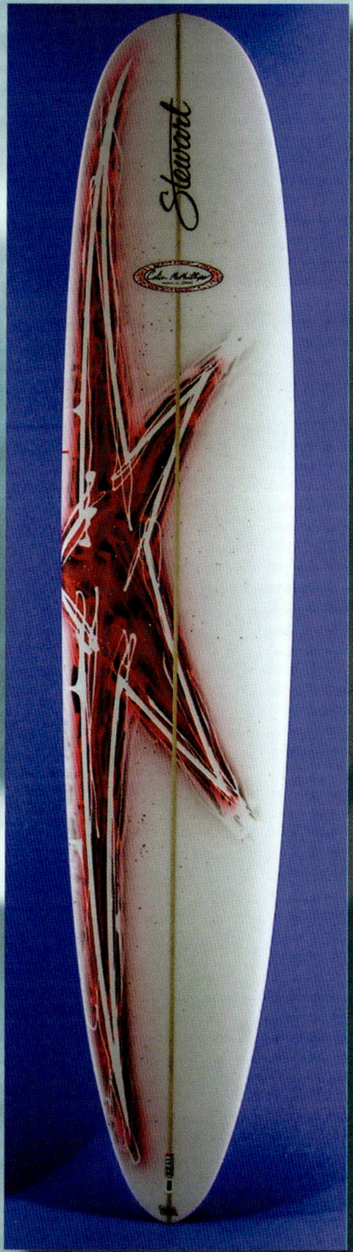

Photo by kind permission of Seabase Ltd.

10', Malibu, 2005. $1000.

6'6", swallow tail, 2005. $600.

Photo by kind permission of Seabase Ltd.

Photo by kind permission of Seabase Ltd.

6'4", swallow tail, 2005. $600.

Photo by kind permission of Seabase Ltd.

6'5", swallow tail, 2005. $600.

Photo by kind permission of Seabase Ltd.

9'8", Mal, 2005. $1000.

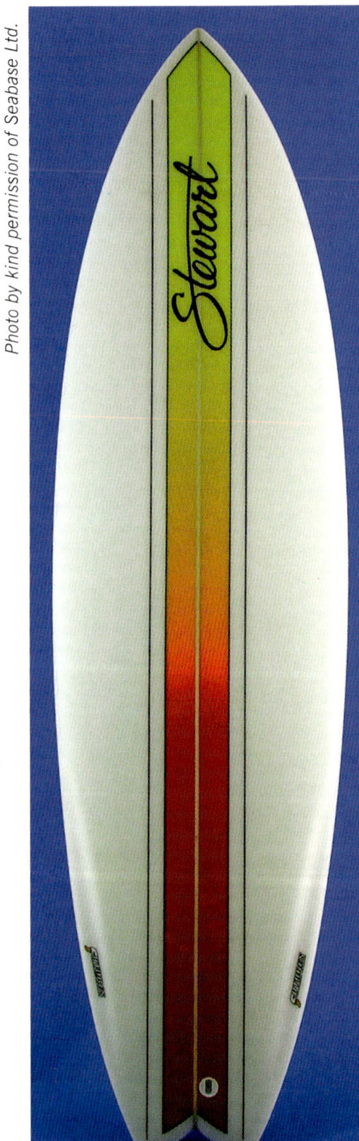

Photo by kind permission of Seabase Ltd.

6'2", swallow tail, 2005. $500.

9'6", nose rider, 2005. $900.

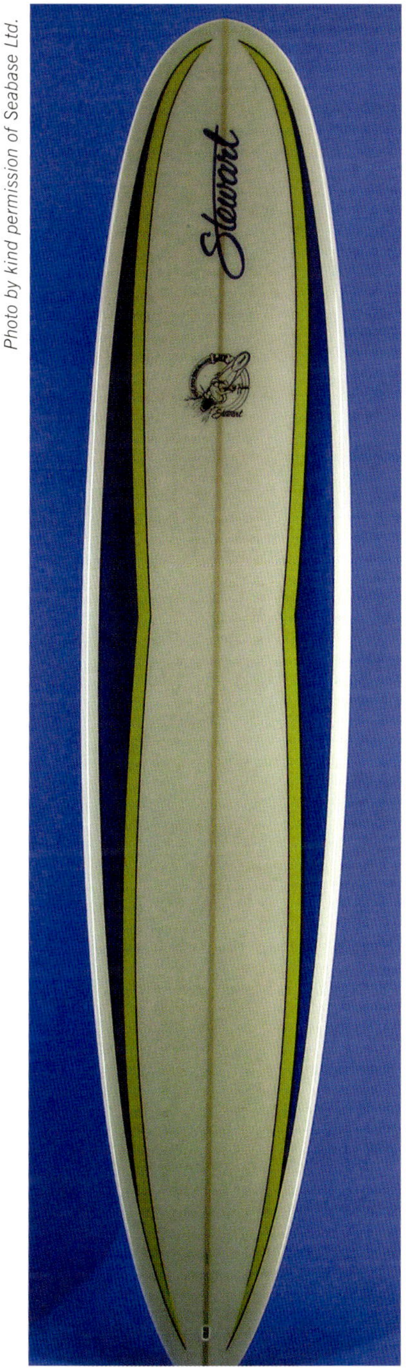

10', Cruiser, 2005. $900.

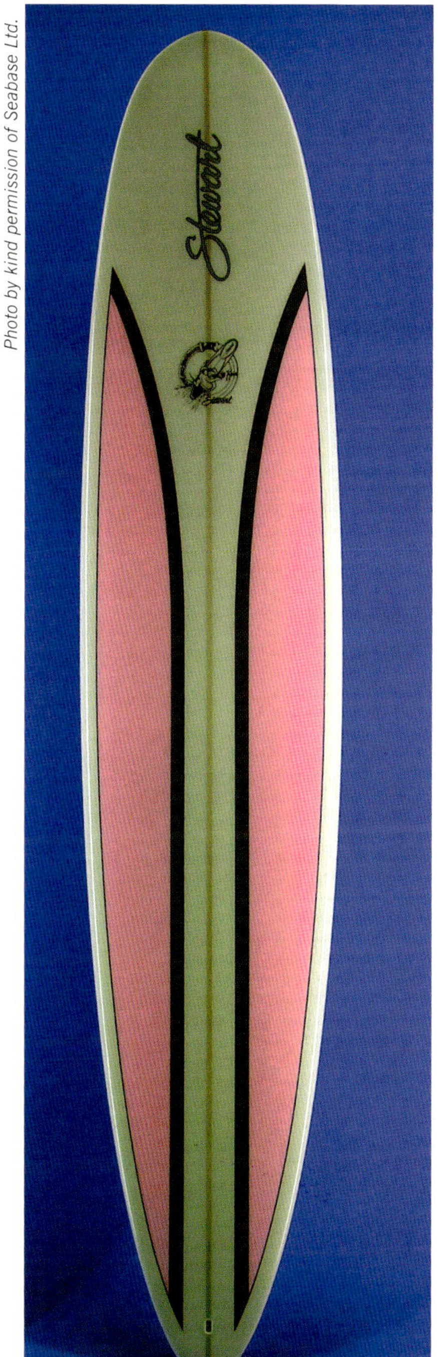

9'6", Mal, square tail, 2005. $900.

9'3", Mal, square tail, 2005. $900.

Photo by kind permission cf Seabase Ltd.

6'6", pin tail, 2005. $600.

9'6", Mal, soft square tail, 2005. $1000.

Photo by kind permission of Seabase Ltd.

Photo by kind permission of Seabase Ltd.

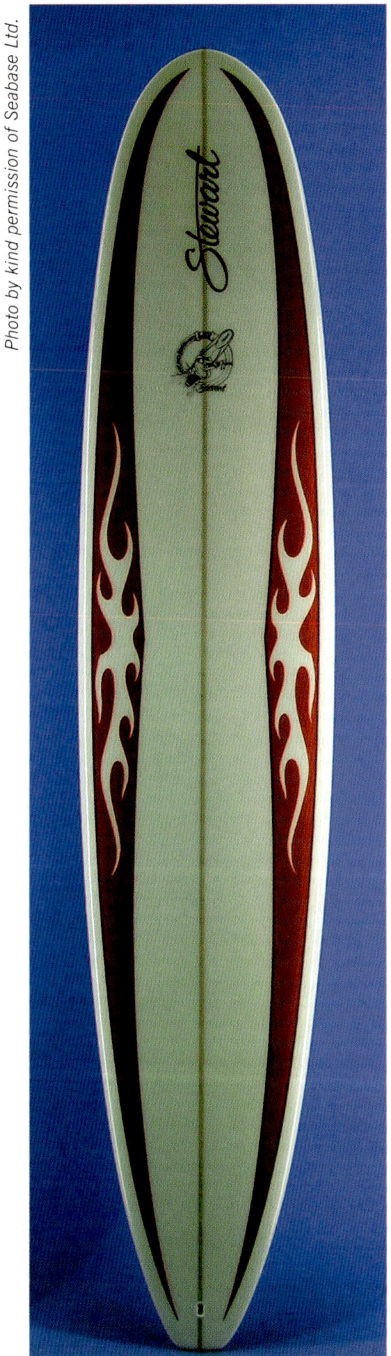

10', Mal, soft square tail, 2005. $1000.

Photo by kind permission of Seabase Ltd.

9'8", triple stringer, Mal, 2005. $1700.

Photo by kind permission of Seabase Ltd.

6'6", pin tail, 2005. $600.

Photo by kind permission of Seabase Ltd.

6'6", pin tail, 2005. $600.

Photo by kind permission of Seabase Ltd.

6'3", pin tail, 2005. $600.

Photo by kind permission of Seabase Ltd.

6'4", swallow tail, 2005. $700.

Photo by kind permission of Seabase Ltd.

6'7", swallow tail, 2005. $500.

Photo by kind permission of Seabase Ltd.

9'10", Mal, square tail, 2005. $1200.

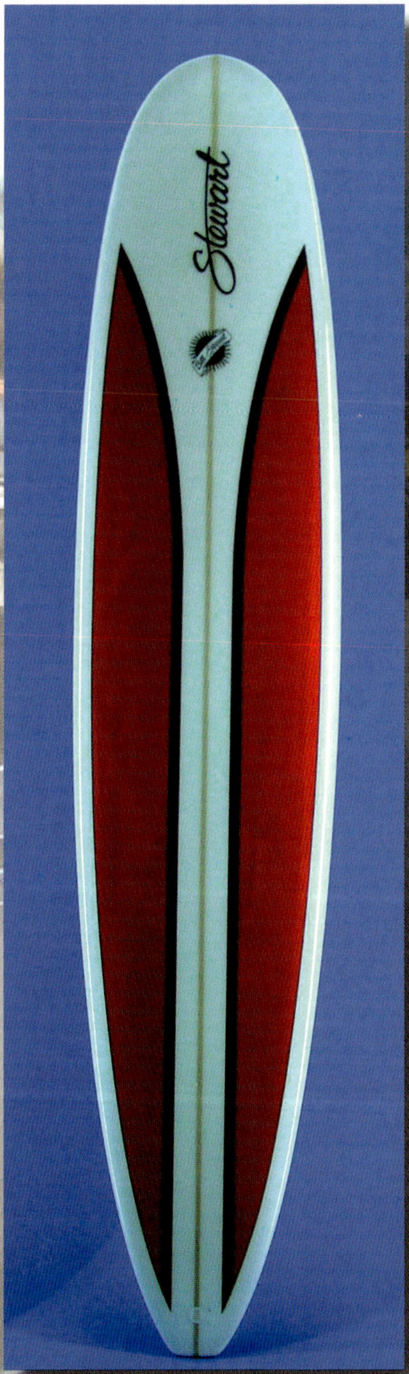

Photo by kind permission of Seabase Ltd.

9'6", Mal, pin tail, 2005. $900.

Photo by kind permission of Seabase Ltd.

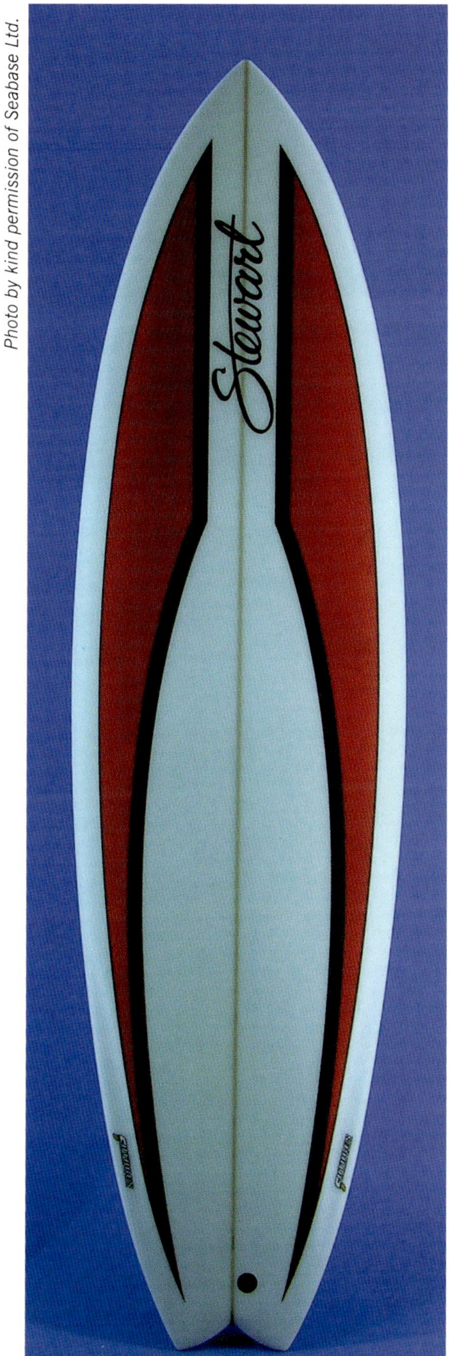

6'4", swallow tail, 2005. $500.

Photo by kind permission of Seabase Ltd.

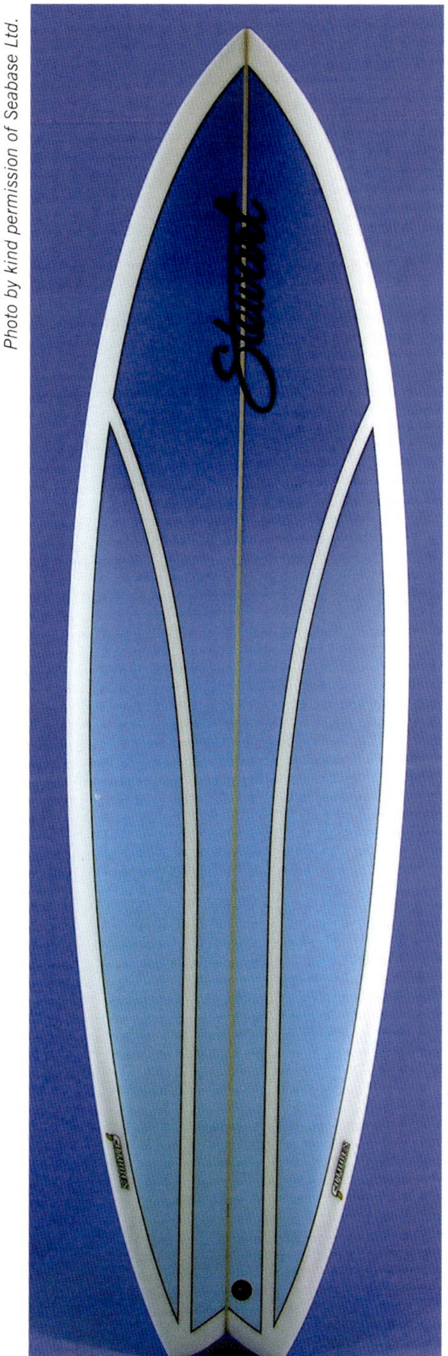

6'4", swallow tail, 2005. $600.

Photo by kind permission of Seabase Ltd.

6'8", swallow tail, 2005. $800.

Photo by kind permission of Seabase Ltd.

6'7", swallow tail, 2005. $700.

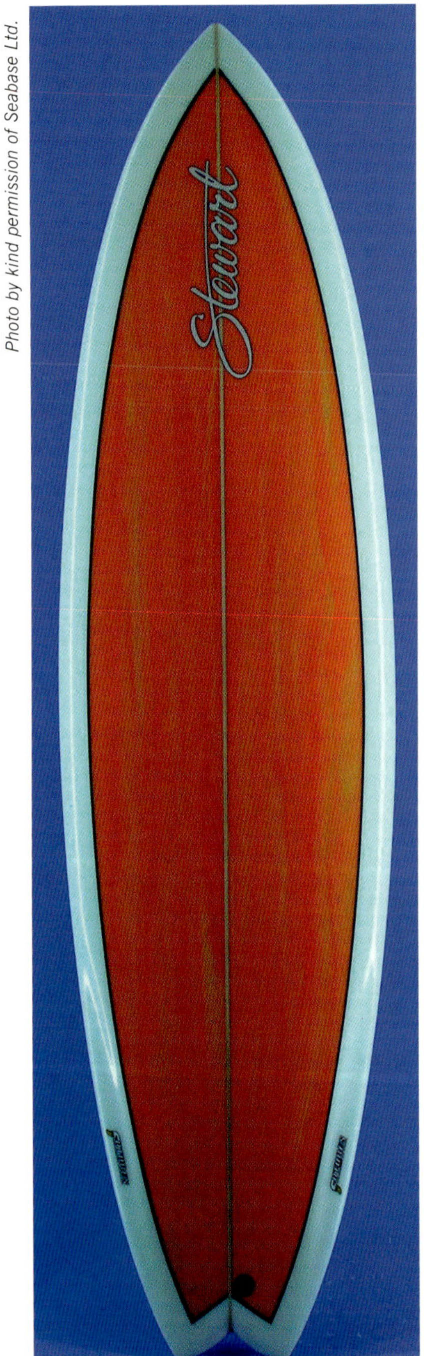

Photo by kind permission of Seabase Ltd.

6'6", swallow tail, 2005. $600.

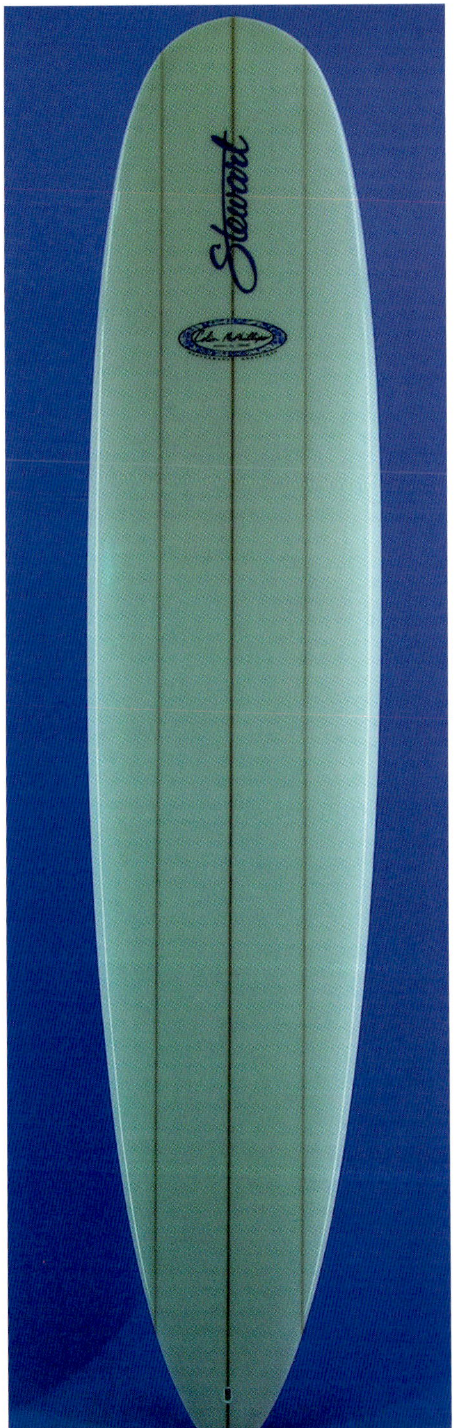

Photo by kind permission of Seabase Ltd.

9'10", triple stringer, 2005. $1000.

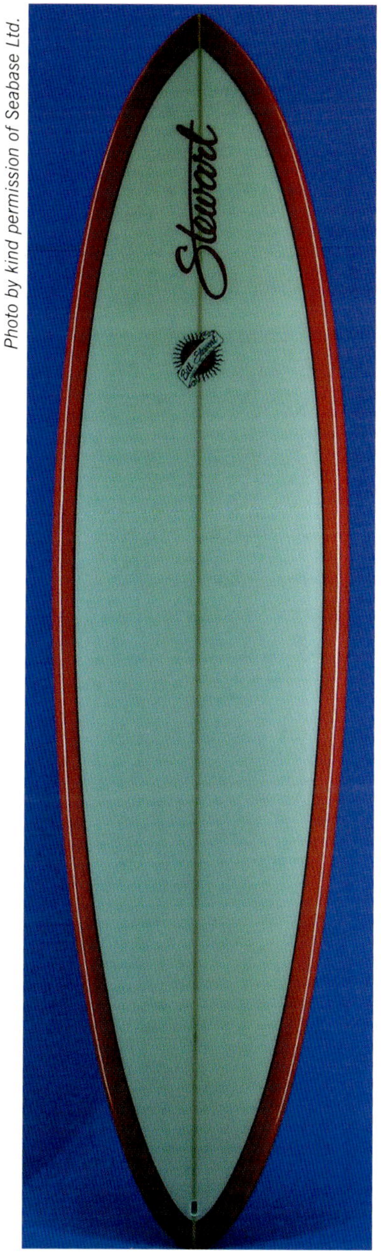

Photo by kind permission of Seabase Ltd.

6'4", pin tail, 2005. $600.

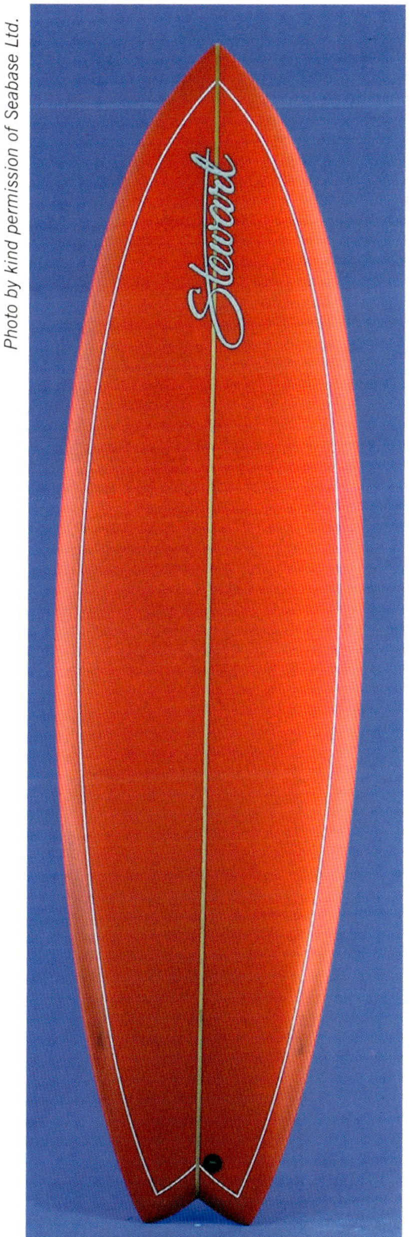

Photo by kind permission of Seabase Ltd.

6'3", swallow tail, 2005. $600.

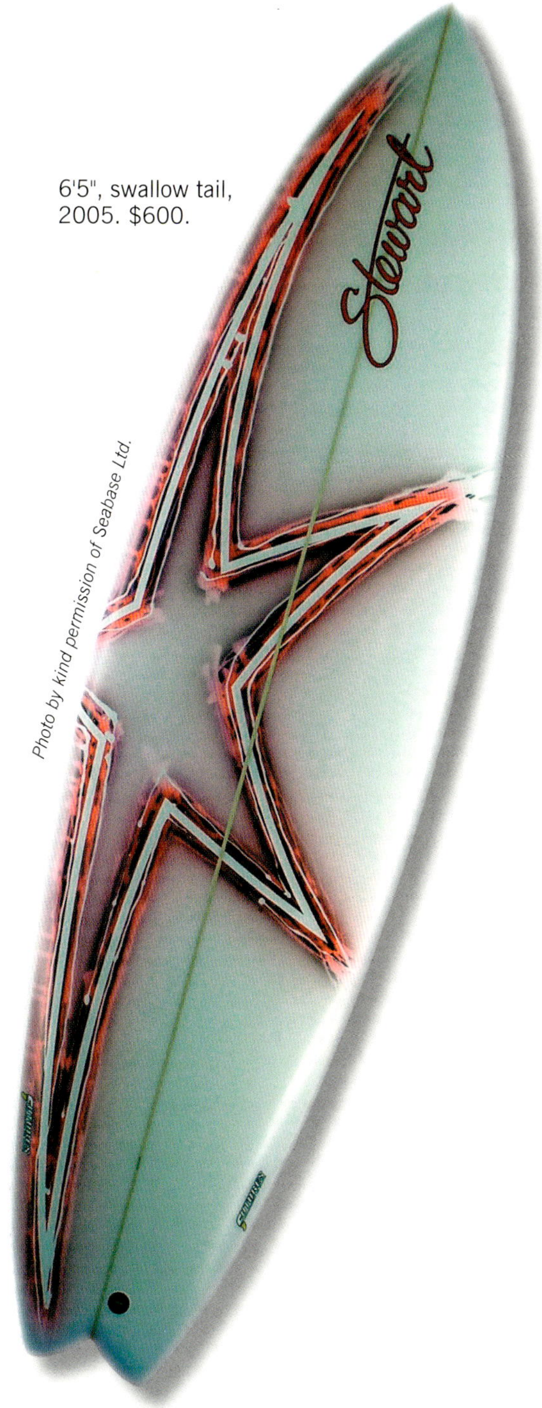

Photo by kind permission of Seabase Ltd.

6'5", swallow tail, 2005. $600.

Photo by kind permission of Seabase Ltd.

9'6", Mal, pin tail, 2005. $900.

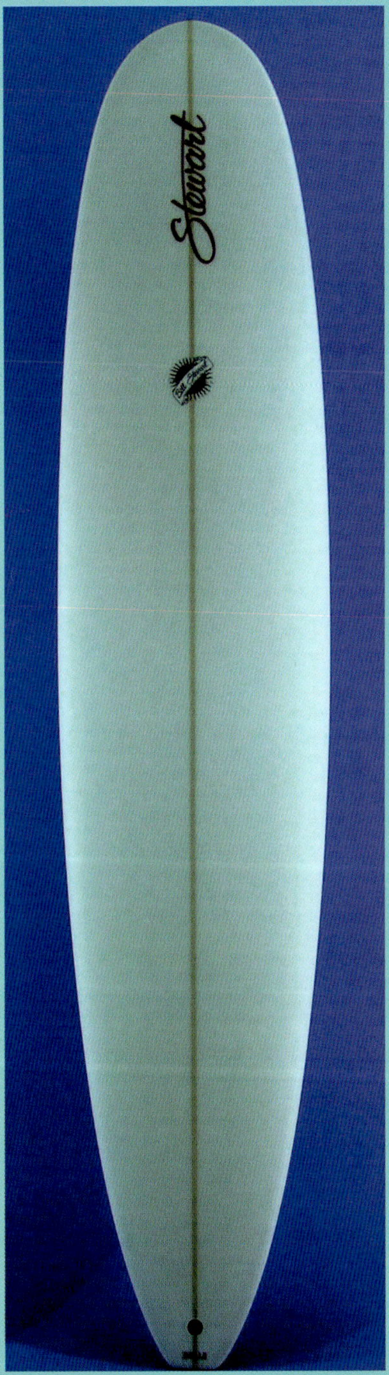

Photo by kind permission of Seabase Ltd.

9'8", Mal, swallow tail, 2005. $900.

Photo by kind permission of Seabase Ltd.

6'5", swallow tail, 2005. $500.

Photo by kind permission of Seabase Ltd.

6'3", swallow tail, 2005. $600.

Photo by kind permission of Seabase Ltd.

6'6", swallow tail, 2005. $600.

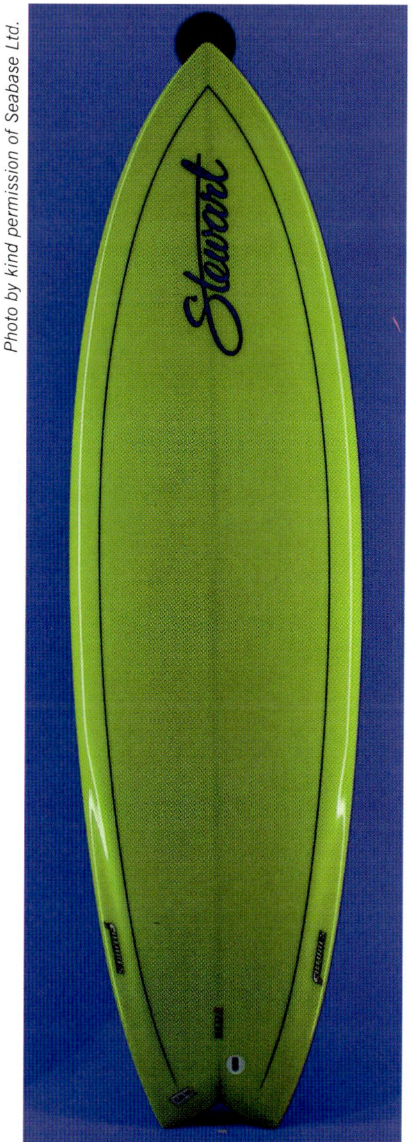

Photo by kind permission of Seabase Ltd.

6'2", swallow tail, 2005. $600.

Photo by kind permission of Seabase Ltd.

6'0", swallow tail, 2005. $500.

Steve Walden Surfboards

Photo courtesy of Steve Walden, Walden Surfboards.

9'6", multi, 2005. $1000.

Photo courtesy of Steve Walden, Walden Surfboards.

9', 2005. $700.

Hawaii

Honolua Underground Surfboards

Photo courtesy of Mark D. Anderson & Renae' Lani Anderson

Mark and Renae' Anderson family at home.

6'8", square tail, 2004. $400.

Photo courtesy of Mark D. Anderson & Renae' Lani Anderson

Photo courtesy of Mark D. Anderson & Renae' Lani Anderson

Photo courtesy of Mark D. Anderson & Renae' Lani Anderson

5'10", square tail. 2004. $300.

Down the line, John Sumpter.

Kimo Greene Surfboards

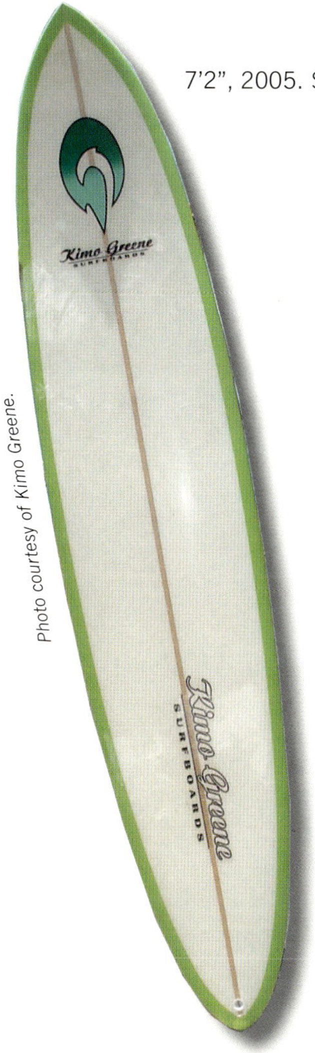

7'2", 2005. $600.

Photo courtesy of Kimo Greene.

Photo courtesy of Kimo Greene.

Photo courtesy of Kimo Greene.

6'4", 2006. $600.

Photo courtesy of Kimo Greene.

9'3", 2005. $900.

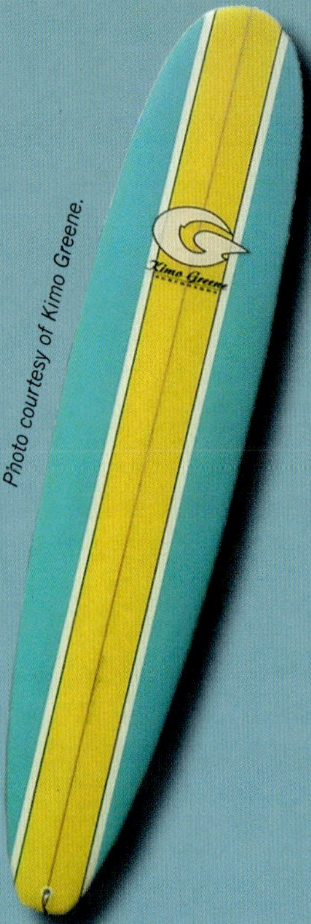

Photo courtesy of Kimo Greene.

9'8", 2004. $800

Photo courtesy of Kimo Greene.

10', 2004. $900.

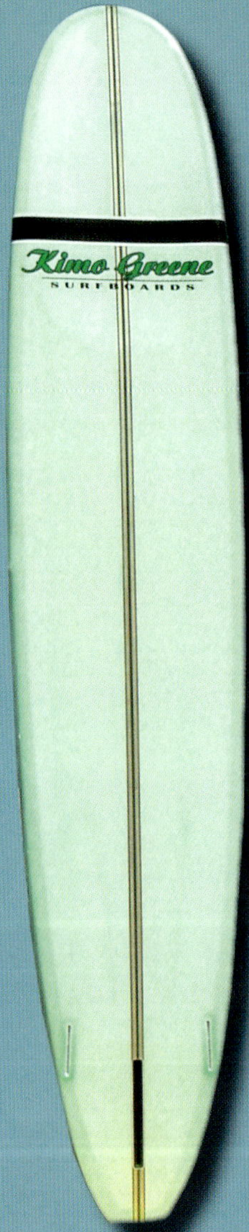

Photo courtesy of Kimo Greene.

9'10", nose rider, 2005. $1000.

Photo courtesy of Kimo Greene.

6'8", 2005. $500.

Kimo goes surfing.

Canada

MacDuff Surfboards

Photo courtesy of Pirate Boards, G. MacDuff.

5'6", swallow tail, 1999. $500.

Photo courtesy of Pirate Boards, G. MacDuff.

6'6", pin tail, 2004. $600.

Australia

Josh Dowling Surfboards

7'4" gun, 2004.
$2500.

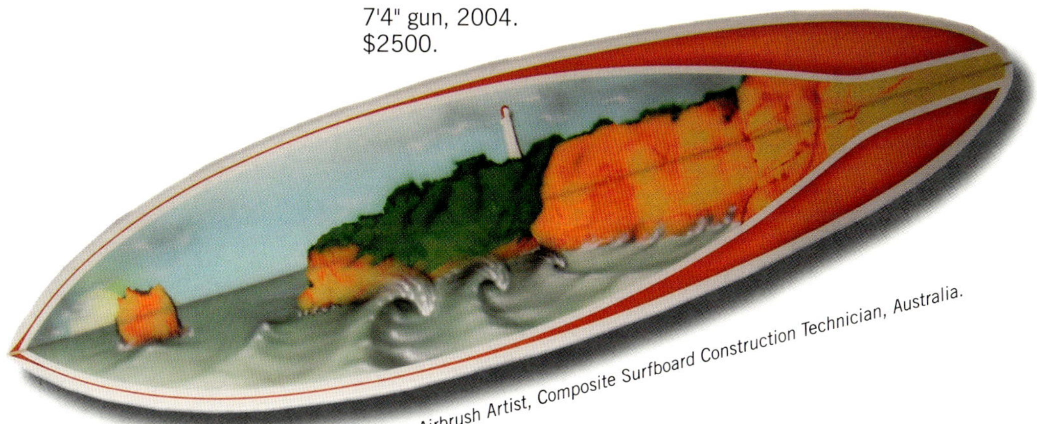

Photos courtesy of Josh Dowling, Shaper, Airbrush Artist, Composite Surfboard Construction Technician, Australia.

Please note that some of these surfboard images were taken from unusual angles by the artist, which intentionally changes the perspective.

Photo courtesy of Josh Dowling, Australia.

6'6", 2.7-Greene Astro, 2005. $1100.

Photo courtesy of Josh Dowling, Australia.

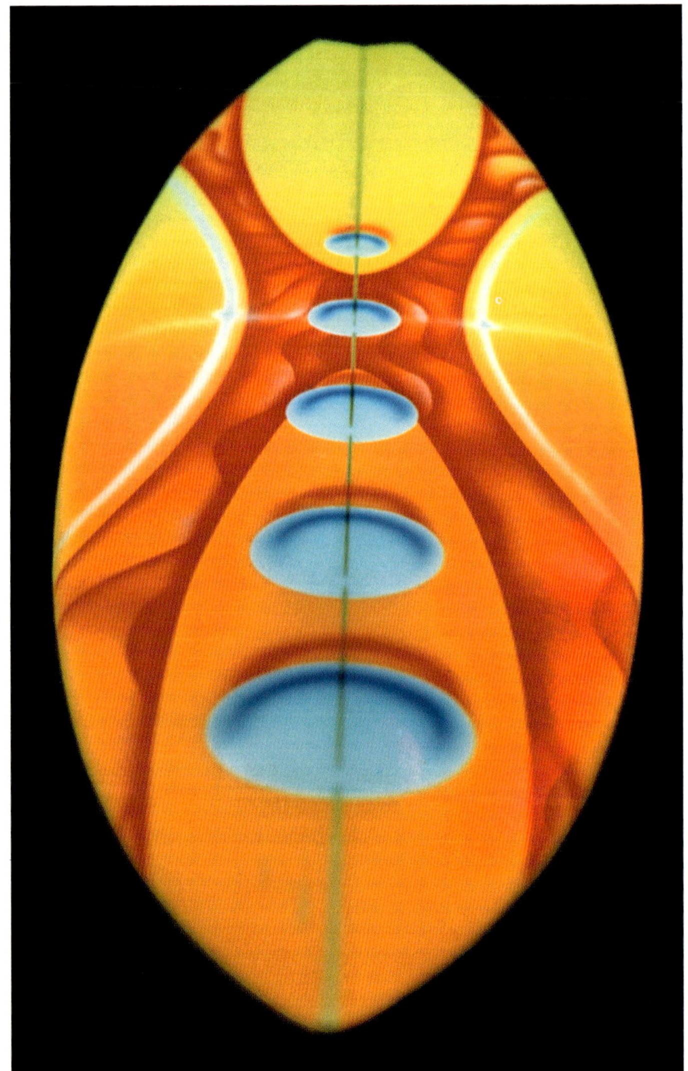

6'8", 2.28-Void Lo-Mo, 2004. $1400.

6'4", 6.2-Bubbly-1, 2005. $600.

Photo courtesy of Josh Dowling, Australia.

Photo courtesy of Josh Dowling, Australia.

7', 6.2-Bubbly-1 gun, 2004. $800.

Photo courtesy of Josh Dowling, Australia.

6'4", 6.17-HH Blue swirl, 2005. $1000.

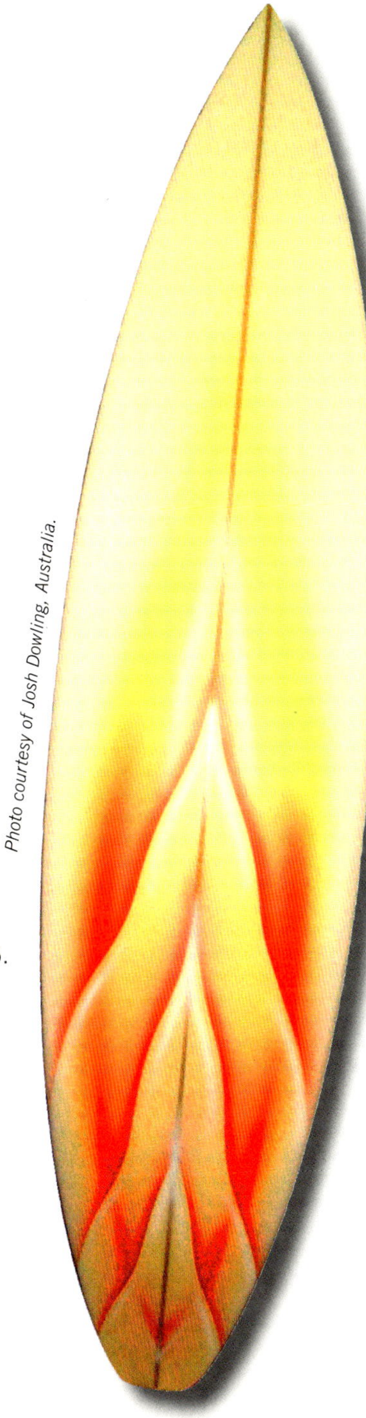

Photo courtesy of Josh Dowling, Australia.

6"6", gun, 2005. $700.

Photo courtesy of Josh Dowling, Australia.

6'2", s2.1-Atom,
2005. $1200.

6'8", 2.26- Tripper Lo-Mo,
2005. $1900.

Photo courtesy of Josh Dowling, Australia.

Photo courtesy of Josh Dowling, Australia.

6'3", JJ-F20,
2005. $800.

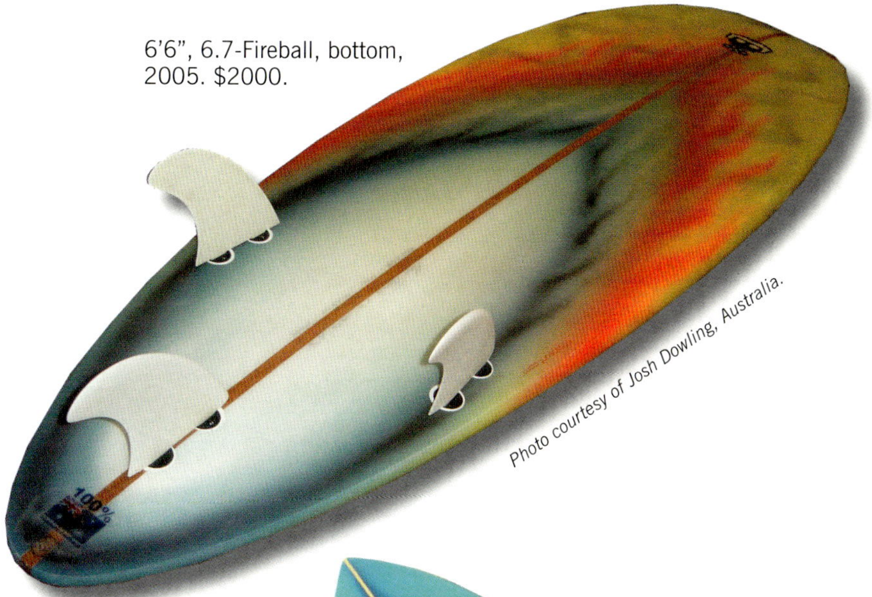

6'6", 6.7-Fireball, bottom, 2005. $2000.

Photo courtesy of Josh Dowling, Australia.

6'10", 6.7-Fireball, 2005. $2200.

Photo courtesy of Josh Dowling, Australia.

6'4", 6.7-Fireball, deck, 2005. $2000.

Photo courtesy of Josh Dowling, Australia.

6'5", 6.11-Hakman 1, 2005. $900.

Photo courtesy of Josh Dowling, Australia.

Photo courtesy of Josh Dowling, Australia.

7', 6.12-Hakman 2, 2005. $1700

Photo courtesy of Josh Dowling, Australia.

6', 6.12-Hakman 2, 2004. $1800.

Photo courtesy of Josh Dowling, Australia.

6'1", 6.12-Hakman 2, 2004. $1800.

Photo courtesy of Josh Dowling, Australia.

7'2", 6.12-Hakman. $1900.

Photo courtesy of Josh Dowling, Australia.

6'4", 6.12-Hakman, 2004. $2000.

Photo courtesy of Josh Dowling, Australia.

6'6", 2.4-Celtic, 2005. $2400.

Photo courtesy of Josh Dowling, Australia.

Josh Dowling shaping.

Photo courtesy of Josh Dowling, Australia.

6'5", 2.6-Grater Vent cut, 2005. $2000.

Photo courtesy of Josh Dowling, Australia.

6'6", 2.10-Hendrix, 2005. $2500.

Photo courtesy of Josh Dowling, Australia.

6'2", 2.9-Greene Probe, 2005. $2100.

Photo courtesy of Josh Dowling, Australia.

6'4", 2.11-Holey, 2004. $2500.

6'5", 2.12-Impact, 2004. $2500.

Photo courtesy of Josh Dowling, Australia.

Photo courtesy of Josh Dowling, Australia.

8'4", 2.14-Jaws Mal, 2005. $2400.

Photo courtesy of Josh Dowling, Australia.

6'4", 2.16-Omega bear, 2004. $1500.

Photo courtesy of Josh Dowling, Australia.

6'6", 2.15-Mobius, 2005. $900.

Photo courtesy of Josh Dowling, Australia.

6'4", 2.17-Psychedelic Lo-Mo, 2004. $2300.

Photo courtesy of Josh Dowling, Australia.

6'8", 2.18-Psychedelic Warp Lo-Mo, 2004. $1900.

Photo courtesy of Josh Dowling, Australia.

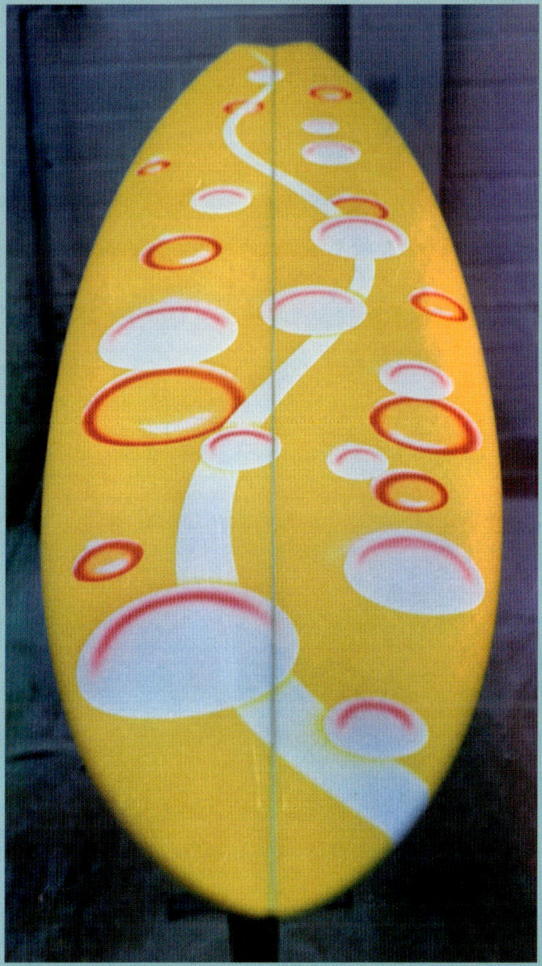

6'3", 2.20-Soda-Pop Lo-Mo, 2005. $2000.

Photo courtesy of Josh Dowling, Australia.

6'2", 2.21-Star Ring Lo-Mo, 2005. $2200.

Photo courtesy of Josh Dowling, Australia.

6’5”, 2.22-Stealth Lo-Mo, 2004. $2300.

Photo courtesy of Josh Dowling, Australia.

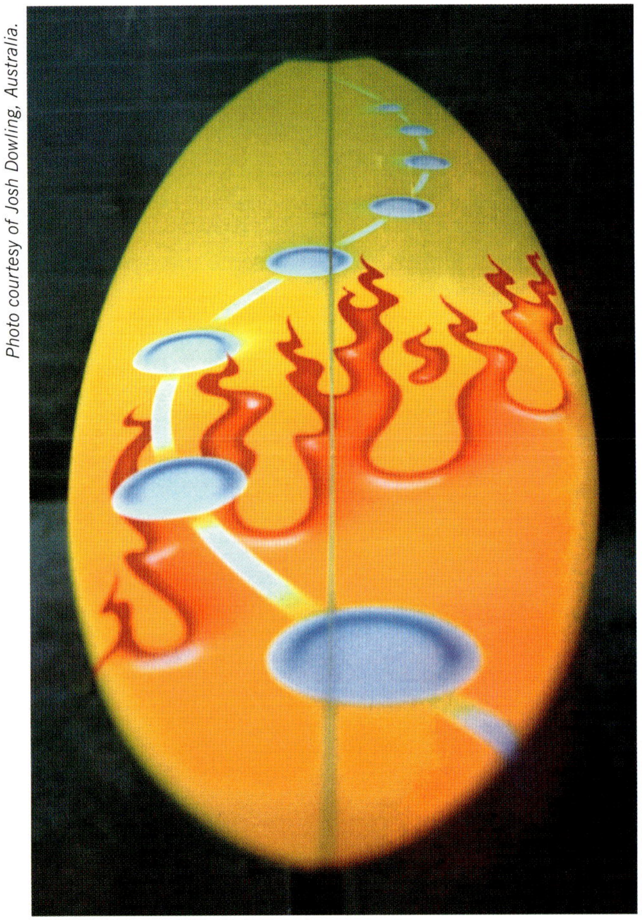

6’6”, 2.23-Stream of Fire Lo-Mo, 2005. $2400.

Photo courtesy of Josh Dowling, Australia.

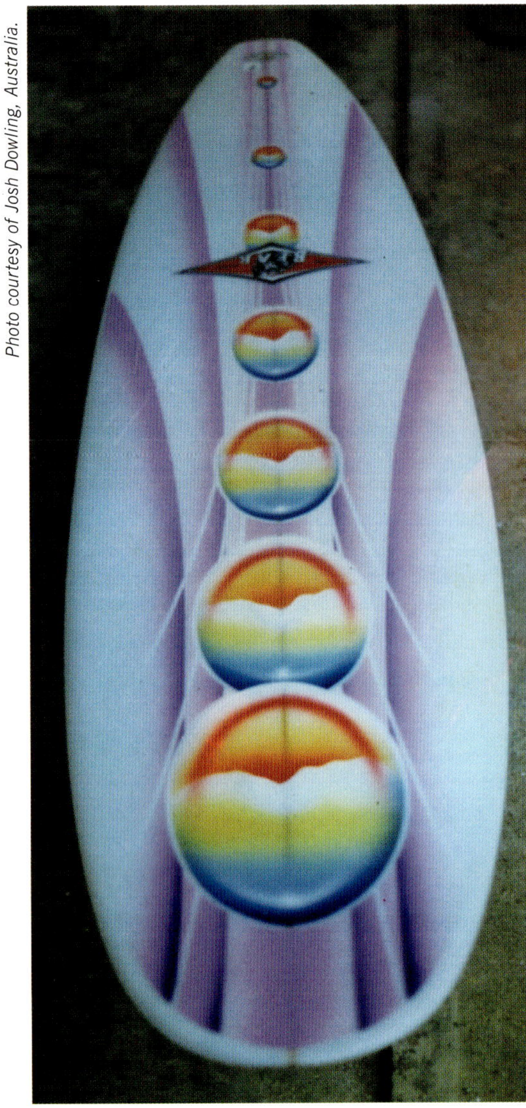

9’2”, 2.24-Sunset Bear, 2004. $2300.

Photo courtesy of Josh Dowling, Australia.

6'9", 2.27-Union Jack Lo-Mo, 2004. $2400.

Photo courtesy of Josh Dowling, Australia.

6'2", 2.29-War of the Worlds Lo-Mo, 2005. $2400.

Photo courtesy of Josh Dowling, Australia.

6'1", 2.30-Wicked Spike Lo-Mo, 2004 $1600.

Photo courtesy of Josh Dowling, Australia.

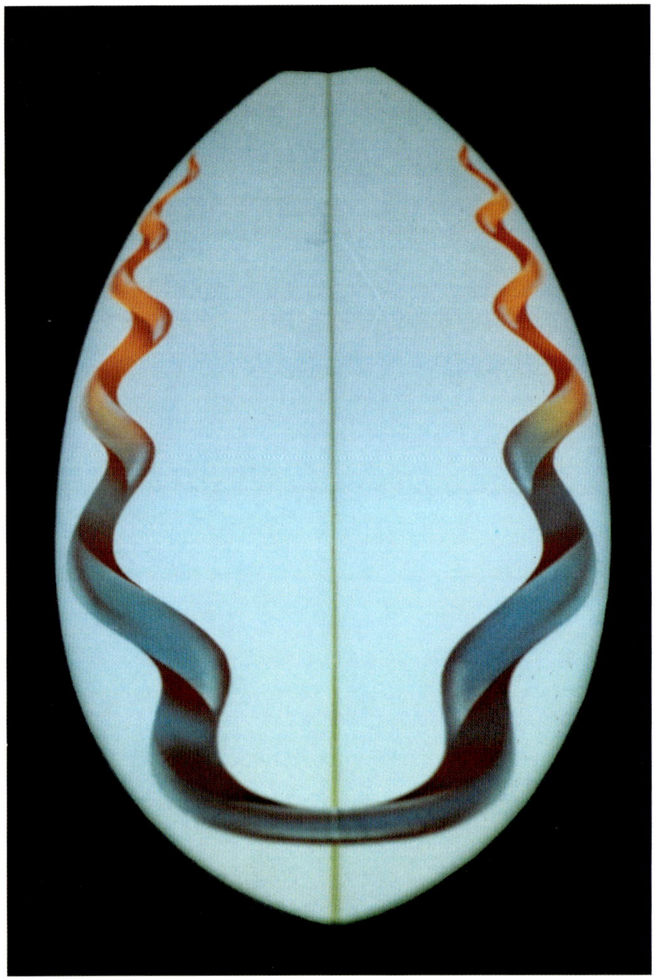

6'1", 2.31-Winder Lo-Mo, 2004. $1600.

Photo courtesy of Josh Dowling, Australia.

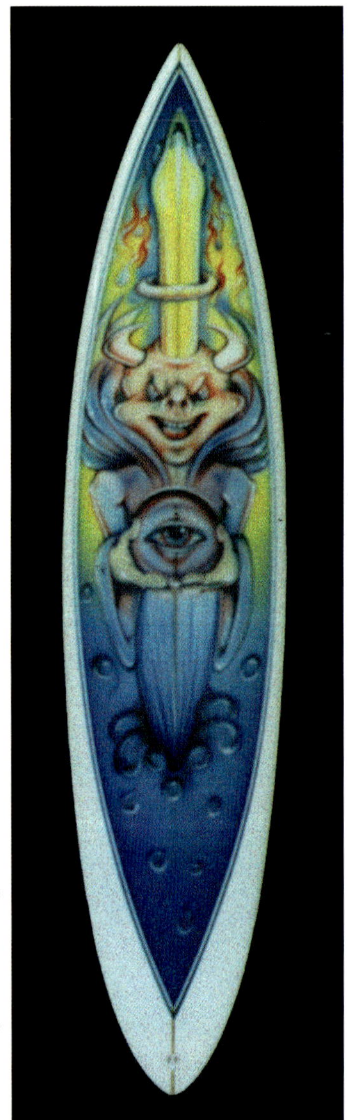

6'4", 2.32-Wizard Lo-Mo, 2004. $2200.

7'8", 3.2-Island Fantasy 2, 2005. $2200.

Photo courtesy Josh Dowling, Australia.

Photo courtesy of Josh Dowling, Australia.

7'8", 3.4-Island Fantasy, 2004. $2100.

Photo courtesy of Josh Dowling, Australia.

6'4", 3.10-JD Lucid Single Fin 2, 2004. $1900.

7'6", 3.16-Lucid Shark gun, bottom nose, 2005. $2100.

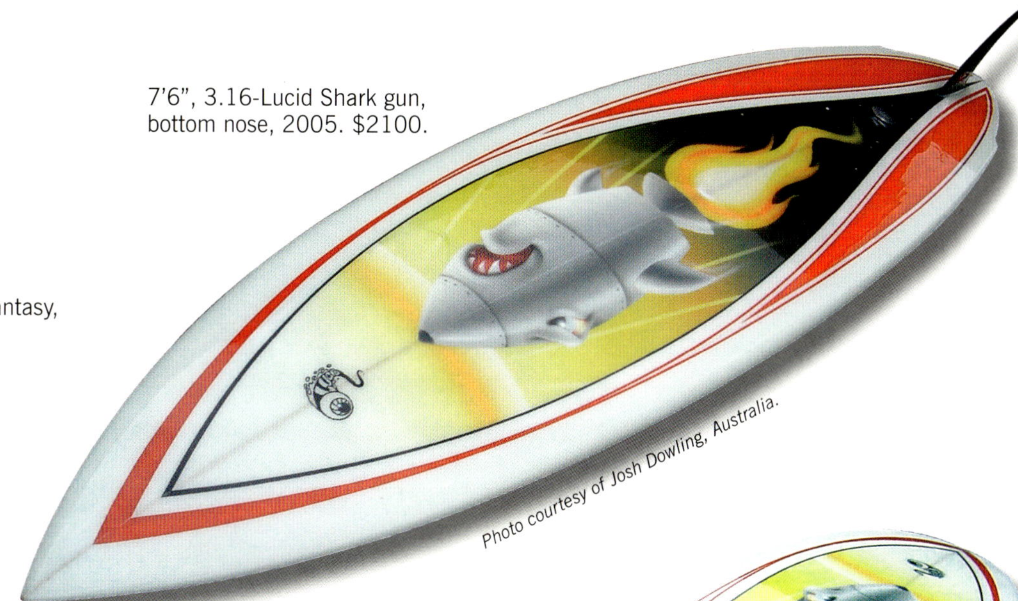

Photo courtesy of Josh Dowling, Australia.

Photo courtesy of Josh Dowling, Australia.

7'6", 3.17-Lucid Shark gun, bottom tail, 2004. $1800.

Photo courtesy of Josh Dowling, Australia.

8'6", 3.20-Lucid Shark gun, deck. $1000.

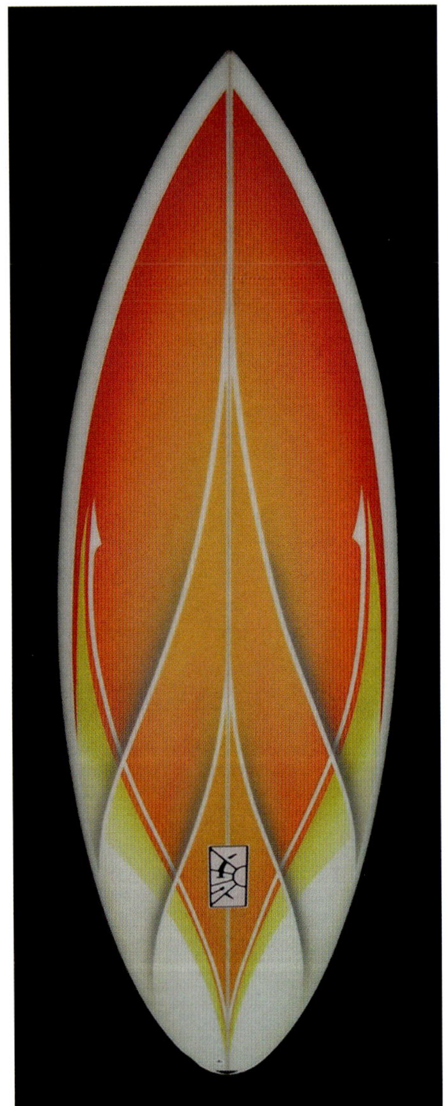

Photo courtesy of Josh Dowling, Australia.

6'6", 3.21-Lucid Tom gun, 2004. $1500.

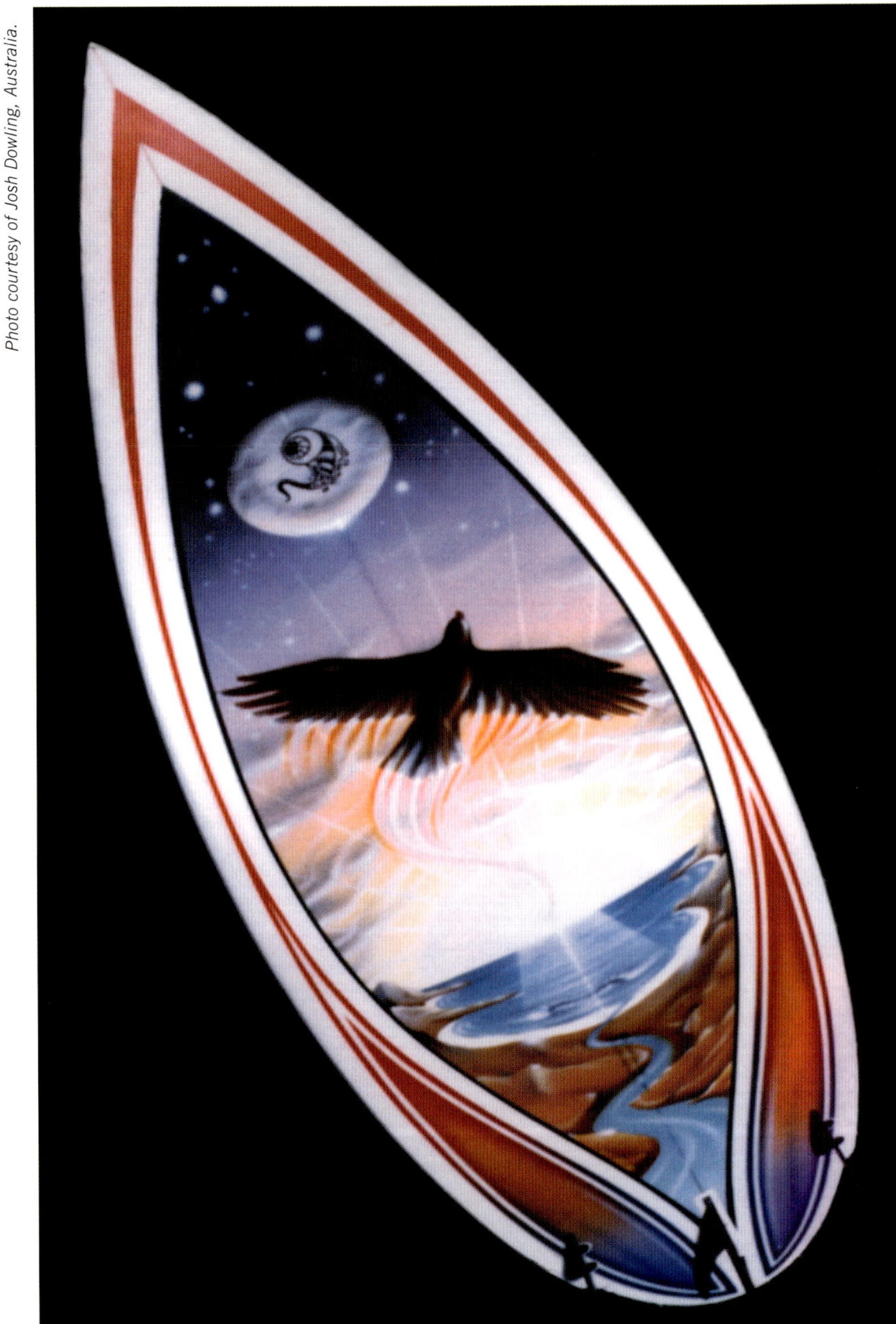

Photo courtesy of Josh Dowling, Australia.

6'7", 3.23-Ocean Flight Lucid, 2004. $2500.

Photo courtesy of Josh Dowling, Australia.

6'6", 3.24-Orange Twinfin, 2004. $1800.

Photo courtesy of Josh Dowling, Australia.

6'4", Composite Flyer, deck, 2004. $1800.

Photo courtesy of Josh Dowling, Australia.

6'10", 4.20-Composite Revolver, 2004. $2000.

Photo courtesy of Josh Dowling, Australia.

6'5", 6.27-Phoenix Deck, nose, 2004. $2000.

Photo courtesy of Josh Dowling, Australia.

6'6", 7.1-Sequence, 2004. $1700.

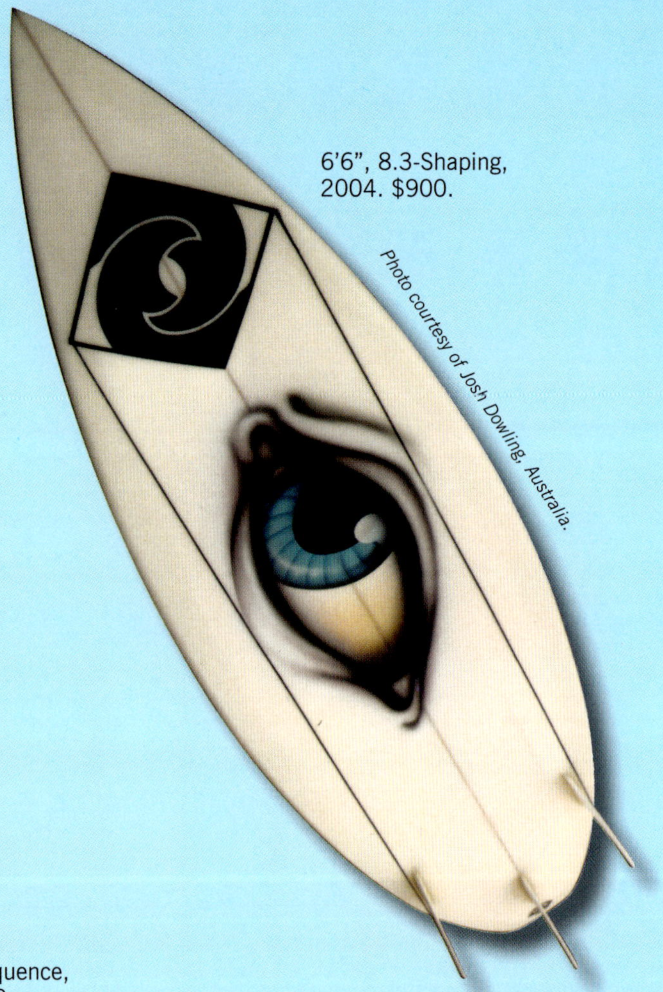

6'6", 8.3-Shaping, 2004. $900.

Photo courtesy of Josh Dowling, Australia.

Photo courtesy of Josh Dowling, Australia.

6'10", 8.3-Shaping 2, 2004. $1100.

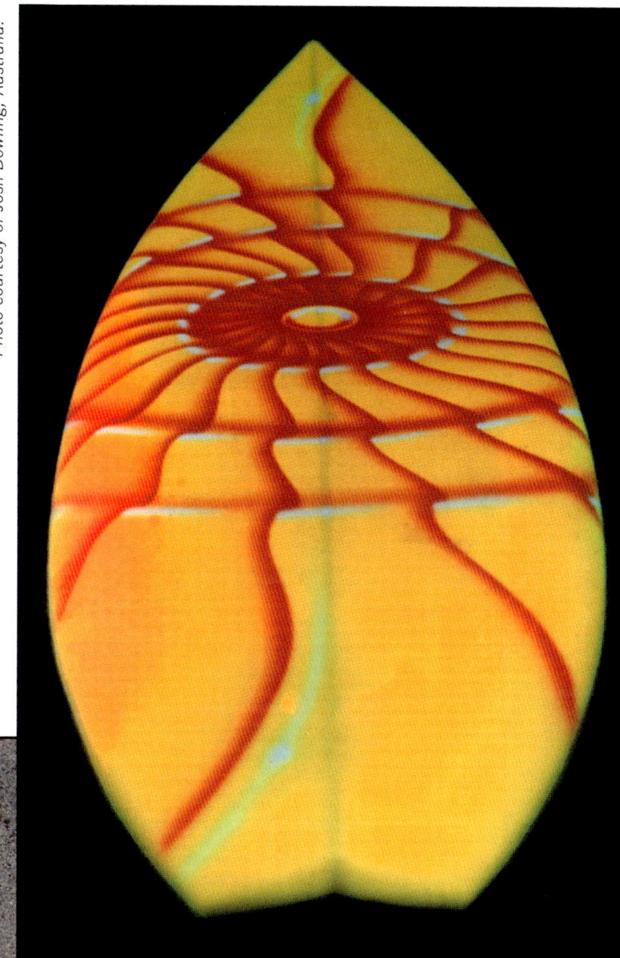

Photo courtesy of Josh Dowling, Australia.

6'6", .25-Swirl, 2 Lo-Mo, 2004. $2200.

Photo courtesy of Josh Dowling, Australia.

7'2", 4.34-Hotbox 2, 2005. $5000.

Photo courtesy of Josh Dowling, Australia.

6'5", 3.14-Jet fish, 2004. $1400.

Photo courtesy of Josh Dowling, Australia.

6'6", 6.17-HH Blue swirl, 2004. $800.

Photo courtesy of Josh Dowling, Australia.

6'4", 1.2-Gooly, $800.

Photo courtesy of Josh Dowling, Australia.

6'6", 09-1.4-Screaming-Bullet. $800.

Photo courtesy of Josh Dowling, Australia.

6'4", 1.3-Roto-Rooter. $900.

Photo courtesy of Josh Dowling, Australia.

6'3", 6.23-Ninja-1.
$800.

Photo courtesy of Josh Dowling, Australia.

6'3", 6.2-Bubbly-1.
$700.

Photo courtesy of Josh Dowling, Australia.

6'4", 6.6-Eagle-1.
$1000.

Photo courtesy of Darren Handley, DHD Surfboard

DHD Surfboards

Photo courtesy of Darren Handley, DHD Surfboard

6’4”, 2004. $300.

Photo courtesy of Darren Handley, DHD Surfboard

6’5”, 2004. $300.

Photo courtesy of Darren Handley, DHD Surfboard

6’5”, 2004. $300.

Photo courtesy of Darren Handley, DHD Surfboard

6'6", 2004. $300.

Photo courtesy of Darren Handley, DHD Surfboard

6'3", 2004. $400.

Photo courtesy of Darren Handley, DHD Surfboard

6'5", 2004. $300.

Photo courtesy of Darren Handley, DHD Surfboard

6'5", 2004. $350.

Photo courtesy of Darren Handley, DHD Surfboard

6'5", 2004. $300.

Photo courtesy of Darren Handley, DHD Surfboard

6'5", 2004. $350.

Photo courtesy of Darren Handley, DHD Surfboard

6'5", 2004. $300.

Len Dibben Surfboards

6'4", 2005. $700.

Photo by kind permission of Len Dibben Surfboards.

Photo by kind permission of Len Dibben Surfboards.

9'10", 2005. $1100.

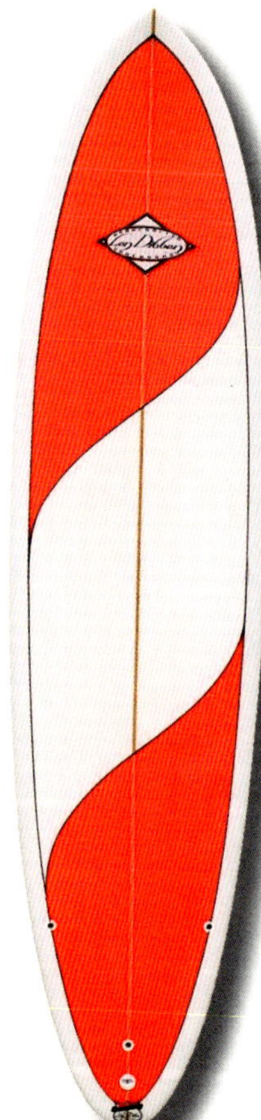

Photo by kind permission of Len Dibben Surfboards.

6'6", 2004. $700.

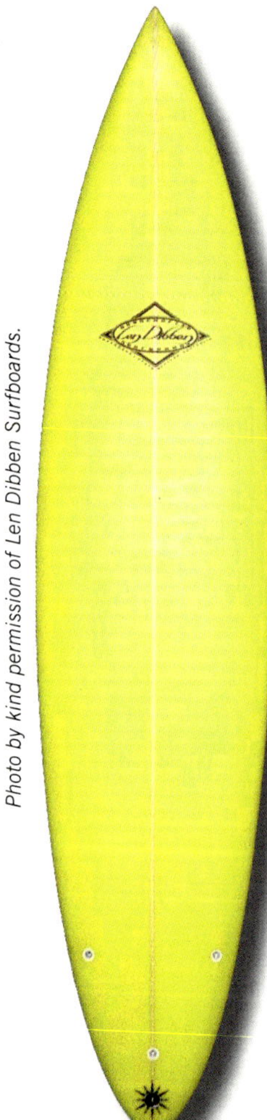

Photo by kind permission of Len Dibben Surfboards.

6'4", short, 2004. $600.

9', Mal, 2005. $900.

Photo by kind permission of Len Dibben Surfboards.

9'1", Mal, 2005. $1000.

Photo by kind permission of Len Dibben Surfboards.

8', 1989. $400.

Photo by kind permission of Len Dibben Surfboards.

5'11", 2004. $600.

Photo by kind permission of Len Dibben Surfboards.

Photo by kind permission of Len Dibben Surfboards.

6'10", triple stringer, 2005. $1300.

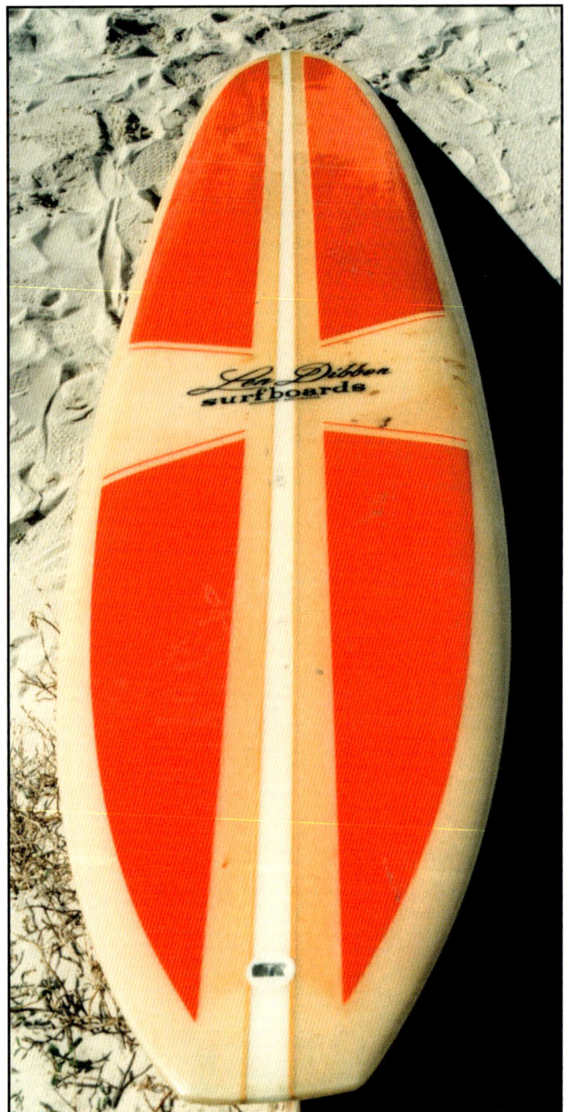

Photo by kind permission of Len Dibben Surfboards.

10' Mal, 2002. $1000.

Photo by kind permission of Len Dibben Surfboards.

6', Vee swallow tail, 2004. $600.

Photo by kind permission of Len Dibben Surfboards.

6'6", swallow tail, 2005. $700.

Photo by kind permission of Len Dibben Surfboards.

6'2", swallow tail, 2004. $600.

Photo by kind permission of Len Dibben Surfboards.

7', multi, 2004. $800.

Photo by kind permission of Len Dibben Surfboards.

5'6", 2000. $400.

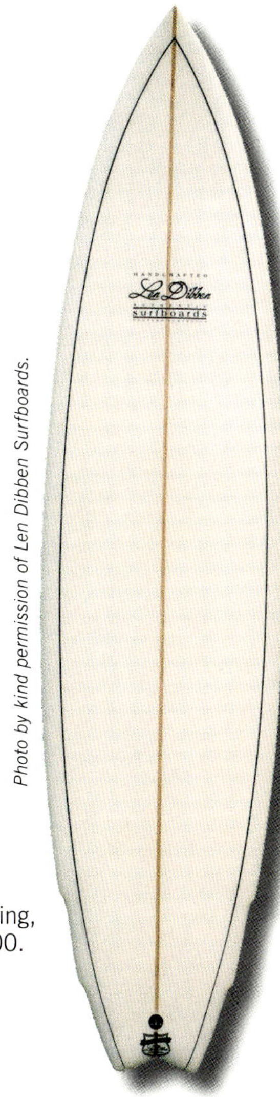

Photo by kind permission of Len Dibben Surfboards.

7'2", bat wing, 2004. $800.

Photo by kind permission of Len Dibben Surfboards.

6'3", 2005. $600.

Photo by kind permission of Len Dibben Surfboards.

6'4", bat, 2005. $600.

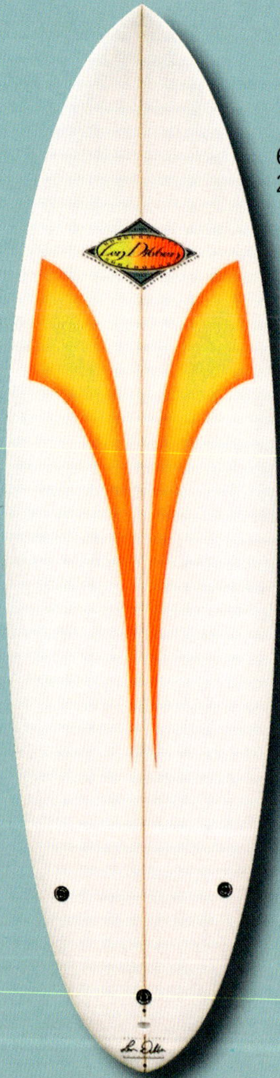

Photo by kind permission of Len Dibben Surfboards.

6'5", pin tail, 2005. $600.

Photo by kind permission of Len Dibben Surfboards.

9'6", Mal tail block, 2005. $1400.

Photo by kind permission of Len Dibben Surfboards.

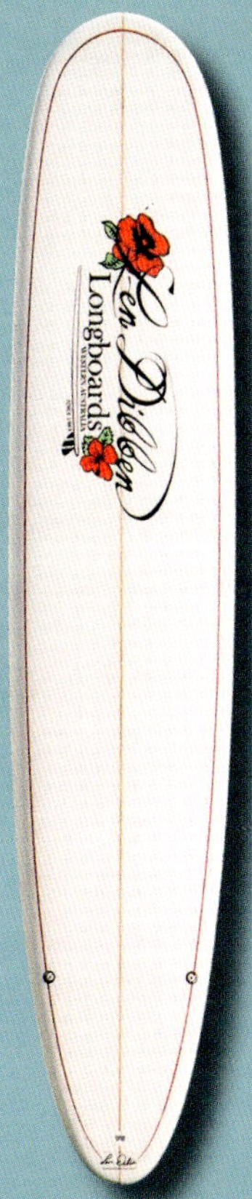

9'8", nose rider, 2004.
$1100.

Photo by kind permission of Len Dibben Surfboards.

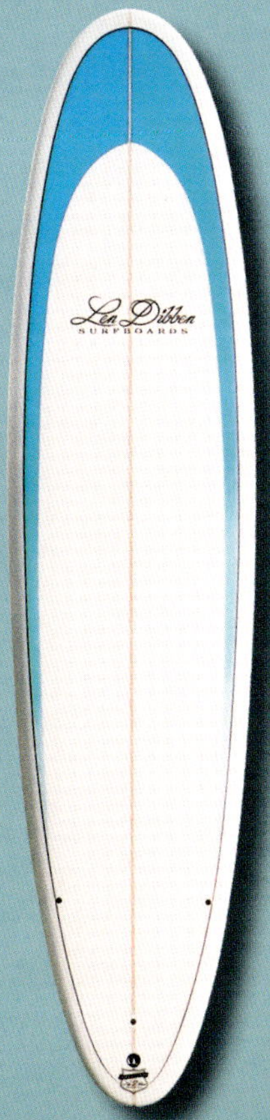

7'10", 2003.
$700.

Photo by kind permission of Len Dibben Surfboards.

9'10", 2001.
$800.

Photo by kind permission of Len Dibben Surfboards.

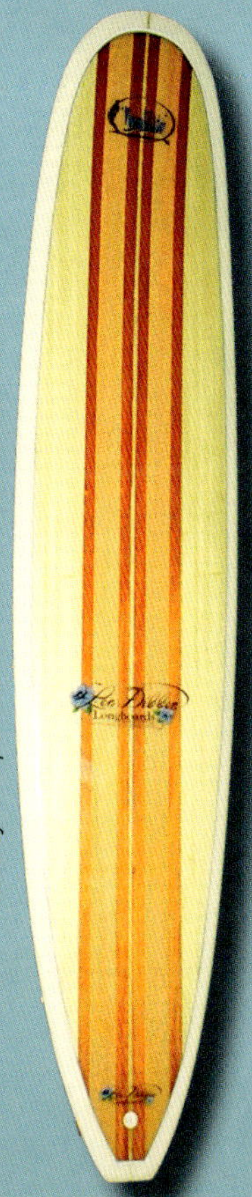

9'6", 2004.
$1200.

Photo by kind permission of Len Dibben Surfboards.

8'2", replica,
1940. $4000.

Photo by kind permission of Len Dibben Surfboards.

Boards at the beach, 1968.

Photo by kind permission of Len Dibben Surfboards.

Len shaping.

Photo by kind permission of Len Dibben Surfboards.

Len Dibben's surf shop exhibits boards from the 1960s to the present day.

Photo by kind permission of Len Dibben Surfboards.

A happy customer, stoked.

Photo by kind permission of Len Dibben Surfboards.

The era of the 1970s and '80s.

Friedman Flyers

Photo courtesy of Steve Friedman, "Surfer Shaper."

6'6" Friedman Flyer fish tail, 2005. $400.

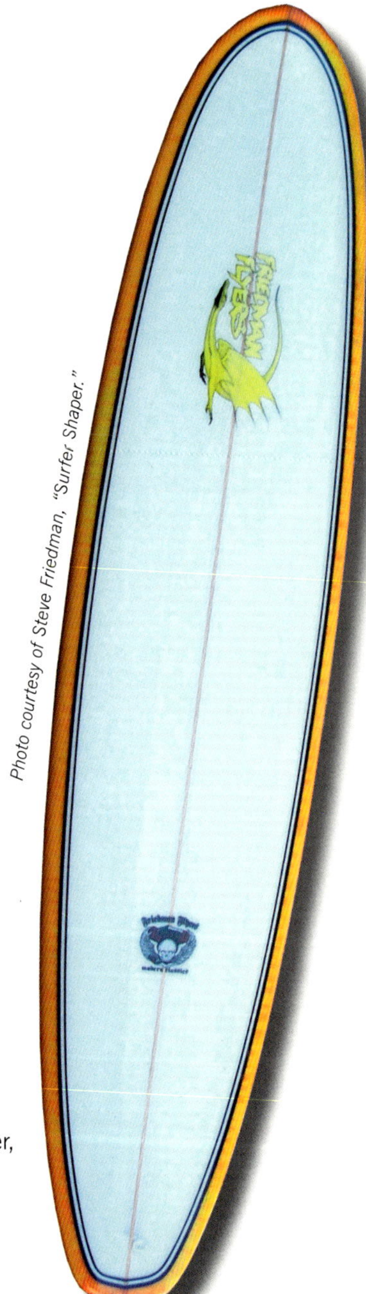

Photo courtesy of Steve Friedman, "Surfer Shaper."

9', Friedman Flyer, 2005. $800.

Photo courtesy of Steve Friedman, "Surfer Shaper."

9'4", Friedman Flyer, 2004. $800.

Photo courtesy of Steve Friedman, "Surfer Shaper."

9'6", Friedman Flyer, 2005. $800.

Photo courtesy of Steve Friedman, "Surfer Shaper."

9'8", Friedman Flyer, 2005. $700.

Photo courtesy of Steve Friedman, "Surfer Shaper."

Photo courtesy of Steve Friedman, "Surfer Shaper."

9'10", Friedman Flyer, 2005. $800.

9'8", Friedman Flyer, 2005. $700.

Photo courtesy of Steve Friedman, "Surfer Shaper."

9'5", Friedman Flyer, 2004. $700.

Photo courtesy of Steve Friedman, "Surfer Shaper."

Friedman Flyer Wood Fin, 2005. $190.

Photo courtesy of Steve Friedman, "Surfer Shaper."

Friedman shaping.

Photo courtesy of Steve Friedman, "Surfer Shaper."

Friedman shaping room.

Photo courtesy of Steve Friedman, "Surfer Shaper."

Five Friedman Flyer balsa and redwood boards, $2000 each.

Rod shaping Britannia model.

Photo courtesy of the author.

Photo courtesy of the author.

Photo courtesy of the author.

Rod surfing the first board he built, a 10' balsa board. Avalon, 1959.

Photo courtesy of the author.

Johnny Mac, Tramore, Ireland.

Photo courtesy of the author.

Rod Sumpter riding the Severn Bore, Glostershire, England. Witnessed by the *Glostershire Post* and recognized as a world record ride of 4-6 miles. *Guinness Book of Records* 1968/69/70.

Photo courtesy of the author.

Rod Sumpter surfing St. Ives, Cornwall. 2003.

Photo courtesy of the author.

The author prepares to ride the Bay of Fundy tidal wave with Surf Jets Surfboards. Nova Scotia, 1968.

Photo courtesy of the author.

Rod Sumpter with Britannia model.

Rod and boards.

Photo courtesy of the author.

Smooth turn. The author at Mollymook, NSW, Australia.

Hawaiian Island Creations

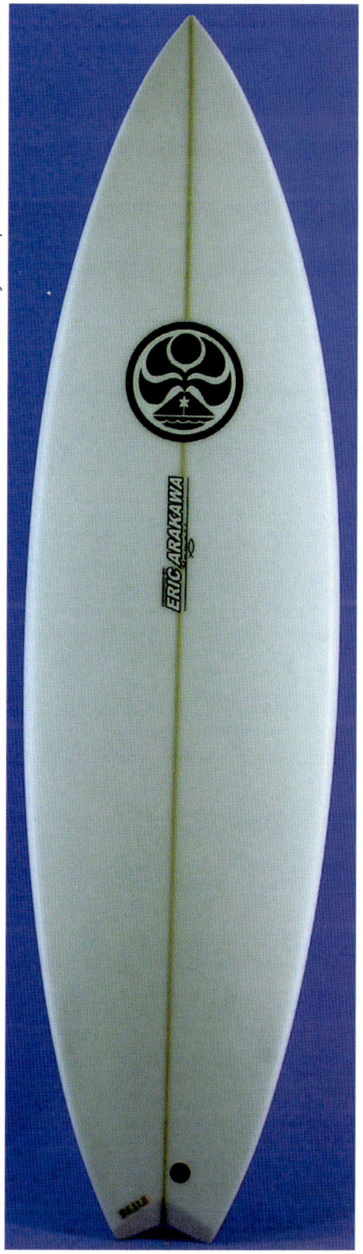

Photo by kind permission of Seabase Ltd.

6'4", swallow tail, 2005. $600.

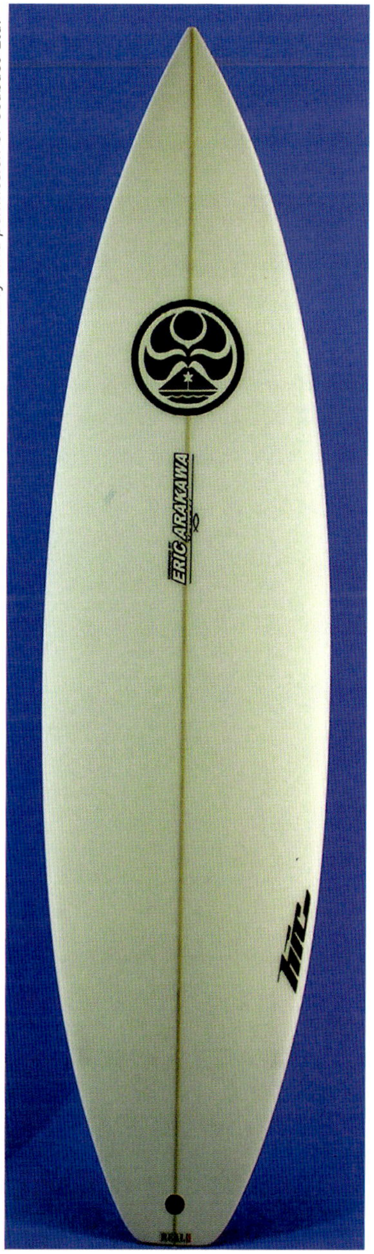

Photo by kind permission of Seabase Ltd.

6'5", square tail, 2005. $600.

Big day at Rocky Point, Oahu.

Graham Looker Surfboards

Photo courtesy of Graham Looker.

5'10", Pig, 1966. $1100.

Head dip, John Sumpter.

Contact Information

For a quote to order a custom surfboard from the greatest shapers in the world as shown in this book, please contact the author:

Rod Sumpter
PO Box 10 Truro, Cornwall,TR1 2LG United Kingdom
Fax from outside UK: 0044-1872 57 1500
Fax from inside UK: 01872 57 1500
Email: rodsumpter@rodsumpter.fsnet.co.uk

Identification of Background Images

Title page: Surf's up. Greenmount, Queensland.

Page 2: Rod Sumpter and Billy Hamilton returning from Keana Point, Oahu, during big seas after surfing Makaha Point, where both rode the Bowl Point and Backwash and survived. Windansea Surf Club flew out from LA for the winter surf in 1964 in a two propeller Douglas DC 3 jammed with boards.

Page 5: Drop in La Santa Lefts, John Sumpter, Canary Island.

Page 34: Tigger Newling kicks out on a head high wave. Water photography by the author while riding with one arm back. St. Ives, Cornwall, 1969 (camera Nikonos 11 underwater camera with 35mm lens f8 250 second. Kodachrome 11, film 25 asa)

Page 42: The author and Micky Mabbot, Avalon, 1962. *Photo by John Pennings.*

Page 49: Jamious Del Agua, John Sumpter, Canary Islands.

Page 54: The author, winner of British National Longboard and Masters Championships, Thurso, East Scotland, 1988. Photo by John Sumpter.

Page 61: Late drop surf boat, Snapper Rocks, Queensland.

Page 66: John Baxendale surfing Sumpters. Cable Bay, Anglesey, Wales. 1967. *Photo courtesy of John Baxendale.*

Page 73: First Hobie board in the Channel Islands. Rod Sumpter, 1965. Water photography, Dennis White.

Page 78: Cribba, Cornwall.

Page 86: Long way to the point.

Page 91: Johnny Mac, Tramore, Ireland. 1967.

Page 96: Surfmobile.

Page 112: Surf's up! Snapper Rocks, Queensland.

Page 135: Taking the power, John Sumpter.

Page 160: Fly away kickout, John Sumpter, Canary Island.